RADICAL LISTENING

RADICAL LISTENING

THE ART OF TRUE CONNECTION

CHRISTIAN VAN NIEUWERBURGH
AND ROBERT BISWAS-DIENER

BK

Berrett–Koehler Publishers, Inc.

Berrett-Koehler Publishers, Inc.
1333 Broadway, Suite P100
Oakland, CA 94612–1921
Tel: (510) 817–2277
Fax: (510) 817–2278
bkconnection.com

ORDERING INFORMATION

Quantity sales. Special discounts are available on quantity purchases by corporations, associations, and others. For details, please go to bkconnection.com to see our bulk discounts or contact bookorders@bkpub.com for more information.
Individual sales. Berrett-Koehler publications are available through most bookstores. They can also be ordered directly from Berrett-Koehler: Tel: (800) 929–2929; Fax: (802) 864–7626; bkconnection.com.
Orders for college textbook / course adoption use. Please contact Berrett-Koehler: Tel: (800) 929–2929; Fax: (802) 864–7626.

Distributed to the US trade and internationally by Penguin Random House Publisher Services.

Berrett-Koehler and the BK logo are registered trademarks of Berrett-Koehler Publishers, Inc.

Printed in the United States of America

Berrett-Koehler books are printed on long-lasting acid-free paper. When it is available, we choose paper that has been manufactured by environmentally responsible processes. These may include using trees grown in sustainable forests, incorporating recycled paper, minimizing chlorine in bleaching, or recycling the energy produced at the paper mill.

Library of Congress Cataloging-in-Publication Data

Names: Nieuwerburgh, Christian van, author. | Biswas-Diener, Robert, author.
Title: Radical listening : the art of true connection / Christian van Nieuwerburgh, Robert Biswas-Diener.
Description: First edition. | Oakland, CA : Berrett-Koehler Publishers, Inc., [2025] | Includes bibliographical references and index.
Identifiers: LCCN 2024037847 (print) | LCCN 2024037848 (ebook) | ISBN 9781523007196 (paperback) | ISBN 9781523007202 (pdf) | ISBN 9781523007219 (epub)
Subjects: LCSH: Listening. | Interpersonal communication. | Interpersonal relations.
Classification: LCC BF323.L5 N54 2025 (print) | LCC BF323.L5 (ebook) | DDC 302.2/242—dc23/eng/20241114
LC record available at https://lccn.loc.gov/2024037847
LC ebook record available at https://lccn.loc.gov/2024037848

First Edition

32 31 30 29 28 27 26 25   10 9 8 7 6 5 4 3 2 1

Book production: Westchester Publishing Services
Cover design: Ashley Ingram

To our partners, Cathia and Keya,
who inspired our shared interest in this topic.

CONTENTS

PART ONE

INTRODUCTION TO RADICAL LISTENING

Most of us recognize the value of great listening. In fact, most people are familiar with approaches to "active listening" and employ conversational techniques such as maintaining eye contact, nodding, and repeating speaker statements. Here, we present an alternative approach that builds on traditional active listening but extends it in dynamic ways. We present a simple but powerful framework for listening that includes attention to a listener's motivation as well as to both the mental and behavioral aspects of listening.

CHAPTER ONE

THE BENEFITS OF RADICAL LISTENING

Perhaps you are holding a copy of *Radical Listening* in a bookstore. Maybe you are reading a free sample chapter online. This moment might feel like a first date—as you try to decide whether this feels right for you. From a business perspective, you might be asking, "Why should I purchase this book? What is the value of engaging with it?" It is also possible, of course, that you have already purchased this book. But even then, it is reasonable for you to be wondering whether this book is worth the investment of your time and mental energy. We are glad that you have these questions. Let's address them straightaway!

To start with, if this were a first date, we would be delighted. You are the person with whom we want to connect. You are interested in enhancing your listening and you are curious—the perfect reader! This book is all about listening and the art of true connection. The basic unit of communication is the conversation. It is how we come to know one another, teach and learn from one another, cooperate in groups, care for each other, and challenge one another. It is how we fall in love, how we convey our needs and wants, how we acknowledge and appreciate others. At least half of all conversations are made up of the dynamic skills of listening. When you listen better, you improve the quality of conversations. In turn, better conversations lead to better relationships.

Now is the time to learn about Radical Listening. We live in an era where connection is sorely needed. People living in many technologically and economically developed societies are getting lonelier. In the United States, for instance, levels of trust have been declining over the last fifty years.[1] In one survey, about a quarter of all people in Great Britain said that they experience loneliness "always, often, or some of the time."[2] It is a statistic that is concerning enough that a Minister of Loneliness was appointed. In addition, increases in screen time mean that people spend less and less time in-person with their friends and family members. Even when people sit together, they can be glued to the many screens that they now access on a minute-by-minute basis. The sense of isolation was magnified by the COVID-19 pandemic and the strict quarantine, social distancing, and face-masking measures. A lack of connection is not only a social issue, it has physical consequences. Research reveals that the increased risk of heart disease, stroke, depression, and dementia—including a higher likelihood of premature death—is roughly equivalent to smoking fifteen cigarettes a day.[3] Better human relationships may be the remedy and Radical Listening is one of the ways of strengthening the connections between us. By listening radically, we can connect with one another effectively, have more engaging conversations, improve our relationships, and experience greater levels of well-being.

A quick glance at your news app will remind you that we are living through an era of increased violence, tribalism, and conflict. There are highly visible armed conflicts in Ukraine, the Middle East, Sudan, and many other parts of the world. A recent poll from the Pew Charitable Trust reveals that Americans today are more likely to demonize fellow citizens who do not share their political views.[4] For example, in 2016, 41 percent of survey respondents thought that members of the opposing political party were immoral. By 2022, that number had spiked to 66 percent. In fact, the Chicago Council Survey found that most Americans consider other Americans to be the biggest threat to their way of life (2023).[5]

Even in the face of such polarization, we dispense with ineffective exhortations about "doing the right thing" and "being kind" in favor of making the case that Radical Listening will be good for you and the people around you. Yes, even as you listen to others better, *you* will benefit from the approaches set out in this book. You will develop stronger connections with others; increase the positive relationships in your life; and be perceived as an empowering and empathetic leader, colleague, or parent. The people you listen to will be able to do their best thinking; feel valued and appreciated; and feel connected to a wider network. The most powerful aspect of Radical Listening is that it is a *mutually beneficial* interaction.

WHAT IS SO RADICAL ABOUT THIS APPROACH?

The word "radical" does not appear in the title of this book by chance. However, we do not mean to suggest that radical is synonymous with "shocking" or to imply that our approach to listening is wholly original. Instead, we claim that there are elements of our approach that are novel and that differ from or extend current thinking on listening. There are three basic ways in which Radical Listening is radical.

First, what makes this approach *radical* is the notion that the starting point for listening is to be clear about *your* intention as the listener. Intentionality is what distinguishes listening from hearing. Is your intention to strengthen your relationship with the other person?

Would you like to increase trust with a team? Are you hoping to influence a group of investors? Do you just want to give a boost to a friend who is going through a rough time? We argue that the intention of the listener changes the contours of conversation.

Next, Radical Listening differs from other approaches to listening in its understanding of what is occurring. Conventionally, listening is considered to be a way of taking in information. Conventional listening is about comprehension and clarification. By contrast, our approach suggests that listening is one of the most effective ways of strengthening relationships and creating opportunities. It replaces the concept of "information" with that of "connection."

Finally, Radical Listening is not passive. It is tempting to think of listening as a reactive act: receiving sounds. Active listening disputes this by suggesting that listeners can check for comprehension by repeating or clarifying what a speaker says. Radical Listening builds on this by adding even more active skills such as asking follow-up questions.

WHAT IS THE RADICAL LISTENING FRAMEWORK?

Before we delve into the practical skills and strategies needed to engage in Radical Listening, let us have a look at the theory upon which this practice is based (please see Figure 1.1: The Radical Listening framework).

You will see "positive intention" right at the heart of the framework. Radical Listening *starts* with a positive intention to listen to people in a way that will strengthen rapport. This intention can present itself in many ways: by treating your conversational partners with dignity and respect; by going the extra mile to understand them; by showing an unambiguous interest in them and the issues they face. The first distinction is whether you are listening *for* something or *in order to do* something.

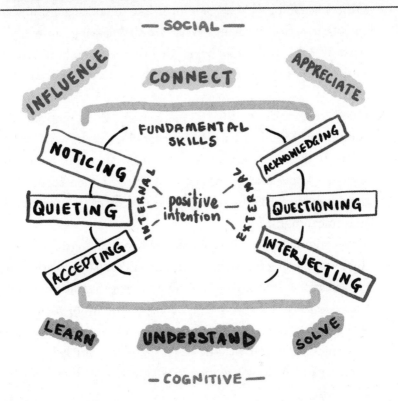

FIGURE 1.1 The Radical Listening framework
Source: Original artwork by Christian van Nieuwerburgh

"Listening For"

When we have asked great communicators how they listen, the most common responses relate to what they were *listening for*. That is, great listeners are aware of what, exactly, they are keeping an ear out for. Some examples:

- Some talked about listening for emotions: "I pay particular attention to how people are *feeling*. What emotions can I pick up from their tone of voice or body posture? Do they explicitly talk about their feelings?"

- Others listen for what is *not* said: "I like to notice gaps in what the other person is saying. What are they leaving out of their narrative? Are there some topics that they seem to be avoiding? I use silences to invite them to articulate what they may be thinking."

- Good communicators listen for motivation. "What motivates the people that I am talking to? I look for clues about what excites them. If their eyes sparkle, or they start becoming more animated, I know that I am onto something. I then spend time digging a bit deeper by asking about the topics that seem to be most meaningful."

- Other communicators describe themselves as strengths-spotters. They are listening for strengths and resources that emerge during conversations. When they hear about strengths, they highlight these: "it sounds like you're very creative," or "from what you're saying, I'm getting a sense that you're highly adaptable." Rather than picking up on weaknesses or gaps in knowledge, these communicators draw attention to what is already there, or what is working.

Not surprisingly, these are all good techniques to use when listening. By listening for things in the conversation that can increase motivation or help others to understand themselves better, Radical Listeners can support people to achieve great results.

"Listening (In Order) To"

Good active listening includes the techniques highlighted in the previous section. Radical Listening goes one step further by being clear about the intention for listening. This can happen before a single word has been spoken. Identifying your intention for listening is the first step of Radical Listening. In other words, knowing your *primary motivation* before the start of a conversation increases the chances that it will be beneficial for both you and the people you will be listening to. As the term implies, it is helpful to know the *main* reason that you will be listening to someone.

PUT IT INTO PRACTICE: TAKE A MOMENT

Please take a moment to think about all the *reasons* that you listen to people. Maybe cast your mind back over the last few days. When have you been in "listening mode"? What were your reasons for listening? In which situations do you feel most connected to others?

Radical Listening is predicated on the idea that human beings have the ability to listen for differing purposes. That is why we have included the common human motivations for listening in the framework. Each is discussed here. We have divided them into *social* motivations (where the purpose is related to human relationships) and *cognitive* motivations (where the purpose is related to support thinking processes).

Social motivations

1. Connect

   This is the intention to build a strong social connection with another person or group of people.

2. Appreciate

   This is the intention to value others, including a motivation to acknowledge their contributions or ways of being.

3. Influence

   This is the intention to encourage people to feel or think in a particular way. As an example, it is possible to listen in a way that can build a person's self-esteem. In another context, it may be more about listening to people so that they are more open to change or innovation.

Cognitive motivations

1. Learn

   This is the intention to take in as much information as possible. This is the mode that is most often associated with students. It requires listeners to stay focused and avoid distractions.

2. Understand

   Currently, this may be the most common intention of listening. To put it simply, people listen in order to comprehend the views, positions, or experiences of others.

3. Solve

   This is the intention to listen to others to gather sufficient information to support them in solving a problem or overcoming barriers. Many managers, leaders, and other people in positions of authority default to this way of listening.

The Radical Listening framework (Figure 1.1) presents the primary motivations in the outer circle. Before engaging in listening, it is essential to be clear about the intention of the interaction. At the center of the model are the fundamental skills of Radical Listening. Some of these skills are hidden during conversations. They relate to cognitive processes within the mind of the Radical Listener. This is why they are identified as "internal." They are presented on the left. The other three skills are visible during conversations (these are identified as "external"). They are behavioral interventions that can be used during Radical Listening.

Internal Skills

The effective use of internal skills is essential in facilitating the social conditions for Radical Listening to occur. *Noticing* requires the listener to be attentive during conversations. When a person is good at noticing, they can direct their attention to what is most important for a particular interaction. Noticing includes the ability to pay attention, scan for information, and determine what is relevant. *Quieting* is the ability to bring a sense of calm to the conversation by using silences and strategic pauses. This involves managing internal dialogue and emotions so that the listener can give their full attention to the conversation. *Accepting* can be particularly challenging for some people. This involves adopting a stance of openness to what others may bring to the conversation. The listener respects the right of others to hold personal opinions and accepts their views as permissible within the conversation. This does not mean that the listener must *agree* with the views. However, in Radical Listening, people should feel that they are entitled to have and openly voice their views and opinions.

External Skills

We also identify some external skills that are necessary for Radical Listening conversations. These will be much more noticeable—they are interventions that you will be making during the conversations. *Acknowledging* is the act of explicitly recognizing the efforts, perspectives, strengths, values, or principles of the other person. When we acknowledge others, they feel seen, understood, and appreciated. *Questioning* is the skill of asking thought-provoking questions that demonstrate interest and curiosity. When used intentionally, questions can encourage deeper reflection, new perspectives, and innovative ideas. At first glance, *interjecting* may seem out of place as a skill of listening. In this case, interrupting your conversational partner is used to show full and enthusiastic engagement. Interjections are used to build energy, strengthen connections, and show interest.

In this section, we have presented the framework that underpins Radical Listening. In the coming chapters, we will consider each aspect so that you can develop your understanding and practice of the skills of Radical Listening. Our intention in this book is to support you to have better conversations, rather than simply understand some of the factors that lead to positive interactions. As a first step, let us make sure that we are all aware of some of the things that could be getting in the way of building better connections with other people.

BARRIERS TO LISTENING

We live in a world that is getting busier and busier! Rather than reducing our workload, advances in technology seem to be providing us with even more things that draw our attention. Cell phones, tablets, virtual reality headsets, and wearable devices now compete with more traditional forms of communication and entertainment to keep us engaged—for almost all our waking hours. The pace of change, constant innovation, and sheer volume of information available can easily overwhelm us.

How much more difficult is it nowadays to have a family meal or a social gathering where people listen to one another? What percentage of those present will be looking at their devices? In any thirty-minute interval, how often will a phone ring or a message ping? To what extent are people fully immersed in the conversations that are taking place? In this context, it is a wonder that we are still able to protect time to have meaningful conversations with other human beings. But despite these challenges, and maybe because of them, it is becoming more and more important for us to enhance our ability to communicate well.

PUT IT INTO PRACTICE: TAKE A MOMENT

Please take a moment now to appreciate a moment of quiet reflection. Even a few seconds of "doing nothing" can feel like a luxury!

LISTENING AT WORK

Traditional views of listening link it with specific contexts. For example, a person can listen to the symphony of morning birdsong, to the sound of an oncoming ambulance, or to the crash of dishes in a restaurant kitchen. Each of these examples seems to suggest that there is simultaneously some common aspect of listening—hearing, for example—as well as something unique to listening in each context. Most of the listening we discuss in *Radical Listening* centers on human-to-human contexts. Typically, this means conversation. Conversations are central to most social interactions. Listening to a manager give instructions, to the questions of a new employee, or to the feedback of a customer are all examples of the importance of listening at work.

Listening, we know, is often swept into that ever-increasing group of competencies known as soft skills. Ironically, these are skills that are important to businesses because they facilitate people collaborating, influencing, planning, reflecting, and engaging in other psychological processes. Increasingly, people within organizations appreciate how vital such skills can be. Often, listening is at the top of the list. But do not take our word for it; research on listening reveals a wide range of benefits. In a recent review, Avraham Kluger and Guy Itzchakov synthesized the results of more than 120 scholarly publications on listening.[6] Here are some of the research team's most important findings about the benefits of listening at work:

• *Listening is linked to better organizational citizenship.* Karina Lloyd and her colleagues conducted a study in which they asked employees to weigh in on how good their supervisor is at listening.[7] It turns out that supervisors who listen well are more likely to inspire people to defend the company when it faces criticism. Employees who had supervisors who listened well were more likely to independently come up with ways to improve work. Not only that, these bosses were also more likely to inspire their employees to want to continue working at the company.

• *Listening is linked to better learning.* It will not come as a surprise to you that good listeners learn better. What might be more interesting is what, exactly, good listeners are learning at work. In addition to learning concepts, skills, and information, good listeners are better at avoiding trouble and office politics! They are also more likely to have more balanced perspectives. In a 2017 study, good listeners were more likely than their poor listening counterparts to be open to considering the pros and cons of a point of view.[8]

• *Poor listening is problematic.* In one study, for example, poor listening was linked to a variety of disruptive behaviors experienced by nurses.[9] These included sexual harassment, being insulted, being gossiped about, being scapegoated, and having their authority undermined, among others.

Taken together, these studies point to an inescapable conclusion. Namely, that listening is important to work. Avraham Kluger and Guy Itzchakov up the ante on that notion by stating it in stronger terms: "listening is arguably a facet of job performance even if it is not perceived or measured as such by organizations" (p. 127).[10] The good news is that Radical Listening is likely to have a positive impact on your professional and personal life.

SUMMARY

Historically, advocates for better listening have focused on so-called "active listening." People who are trained in this approach typically maintain eye contact, check in with the speaker to ensure their meaning has been conveyed accurately, and use the speaker's language. These can lead to better attention and comprehension and can demonstrate investment in the conversation. Radical Listening builds on this and extends it. The major points of departure are twofold: First, Radical Listening places a heavy emphasis on your intention for listening. Instead of treating listening as a singular conversational skill, we position it as an orientation to interacting. This means that great listeners modify their style depending on their listening intention. They notice and convey different things in conversations in which they want to connect, argue, learn, or entertain. The second departure that makes this approach radical is its emphasis on a wide range of internal and external listening skills. The most counterintuitive of these are questioning and interjection. In both cases, the listener interrupts the flow of the conversation. It would be fair to propose that such interruptions could lead to doubt about whether the person is really listening. However, we argue that these skills demonstrate unusually high conversational engagement and can lead to improved interactions.

QUESTIONS

1. What stands out to you as the most radical idea presented in this chapter?
2. What have you noticed in your own life about the benefits of listening well to others?
3. What will you do differently when listening to people as a result of reading this chapter?

CHAPTER TWO

INTENTION

W e start with a provocation: the best listening is *proactive*, not re-active. The traditional view of listening is that it is a receptive activity. As soon as someone starts speaking, it can seem like they are in "broadcasting mode" and that we should be in "receiving mode." It is easy to assume that we should be like sponges, trying to absorb what is being said. To the extent that we have any choice of what to do as a listener, it appears to be a narrow selection between listening and not listening.

In truth, listeners should be much more than sponges. That metaphor suggests that the sponge is passive and singular in its abil-ity. Namely, sponges soak up liquid. Perhaps a more fruitful alterna-tive is to describe listening like being hungry. The process requires a person to eat food but does not place limits on when to eat, how much to eat, or what type of food is consumed. Each meal is distinct and, as we shall see, each listening session is unique too.

PROFESSIONAL LISTENERS

There are numerous professional roles in society that require us to listen in particular ways: therapists, customer service staff, nurses, doctors, coaches, lawyers, journalists, teachers, ombudsmen, librarians, air traffic controllers, intelligence officers, orchestra conductors, and salespeople, to name a few. People in these fields are required to listen effectively to do their jobs well.

Although they all have listening in common, it is relatively easy to see that there are slight variations in their purposes:

- Therapists and coaches use listening to understand a person's problems or perspective. They also use listening to build trusting relationships and demonstrate empathy.
- Nurses and doctors listen to understand the needs of their patients and to diagnose illnesses.
- Teachers listen to determine what their students have understood and what they still need to learn.
- Customer service staff listen so that clients feel heard and so that they can resolve complaints.
- Lawyers listen to gather information to assess the merits of a case and to develop effective arguments.
- Journalists listen to gather information to write accurate and engaging articles.
- Salespeople listen to understand their customers' needs and offer customized solutions or products.

The list goes on and on. All these professionals are listening with a particular *purpose* in mind to be as effective as possible in their jobs. Radical Listening is a way of bringing this kind of purposeful interaction into our everyday lives. What is radical about the listening that we propose in this book is the notion that there are far more than two simple choices—listen or not listen. In Radical Listening, we become active participants in the conversation. To be the best conversational partner possible, we must be *intentional* about our role. Radical Listening is a two-way interaction. What is *our* desired outcome from the conversation? What do *we* hope our conversational partners will take away from the interaction? Perhaps the most foundational aspect of listening is identifying your "why" as a listener. That is, you need to understand your motives for listening.

POSITIVE INTENTION

Radical Listening begins when you become clear about *your* intention as the listener. You can likely recall times that you listened out of politeness, or listened to learn, or listened to buy time, or listened to enjoy. At the heart of intention is the idea that listening is related to distinct outcomes: strengthening your relationship with someone, influencing investors, showing your appreciation, attempting to increase trust, and so forth.

Outcome-based listening has its roots, in part, in a program of research conducted in the 1980s and 1990s on "optimal support matching."[1] As the name suggests, this is the idea that a person should offer something that aligns with the type of support being requested. For example, if your best friend tells you that she had a tense interaction with her colleague, it is helpful to know whether she is seeking advice on how to handle the relationship or if she just wants to be validated for what she is experiencing. Too often, we get this simple equation wrong and listen with expertise (advising) instead of listening with compassion (validating). Similarly, if your friend invites you over and tells you he needs help shifting his kitchen table, it is reasonable to assume that he is asking for hands-on help and not validation. He will feel misheard if you respond by saying, "Wow, that is so tough for you. It looks like you could never move it all by yourself and my heart really goes out to you."

Social support works best when what you offer matches what the person needs. Some of the most common issues, and their corresponding needs, are shown in Table 2.1.

TABLE 2.1 Optimal support matching

The speaker's stated issue	Example	The help they are asking for
Facing uncertainty	Being asked to work in a new market	Information
Feeling bad	Frustrated after losing a potential sale	Compassion, acceptance
Facing a practical problem	Does not know how to operate software	Tools, advice, hands-on assistance
Wrestling with sense of self	Newly promoted and feels like an imposter	Validation, respect, compassion

Although optimal support matching was originally intended to describe how people care for one another, it also has direct links to Radical Listening. Matching social support requires that a person pay close attention to the needs of the speaker and understand their own motives in the relationship as well. You can think of this as listening with a positive intention. With a positive intention in mind, you increase the chances of providing the right kind of listening for your conversational partner.

It is worth noting that simply having a positive intention is not always sufficient to guarantee an engaging or effective conversation. Just as people misalign their social support, we also fall prey to not following through on our positive intentions. This can happen because there are numerous barriers to giving our full attention to others that can cloud our clear sense of purpose in listening. The obstacles to Radical Listening come in two general types. First, there are the internal barriers to listening. These are a variety of feelings, assumptions, and mental chatter that distract from effective attention. Second, there is a set of so-called "antisocial" barriers to listening. These are instances in which our listening is relatively more self-centered than focused on the speaker.

GETTING IT WRONG, PART ONE: INTERNAL BARRIERS TO LISTENING

We live in a world that seems to get busier and busier! Not only do we have our daily work tasks but we also have more meetings, longer commutes, and more interactions with more people in more locations than at any time in the history of work. What's more, the very technologies that are intended to help manage the load can consume even more of our time and attention. Cell phones, tablets, task management apps, email, and wearable devices now compete with more traditional forms of communication and are designed to wrest our attention.

In addition to the many real and present external distractions, there are also *internal* obstacles to great listening. Our internal worlds can be loud. At times, they are a blaring noise of emotion, attitude, and motives that can make it impossible for us to give others our full attention. Let us consider six of the most common *internal* barriers that can interfere with your ability to listen well.

1. Comparing: "It Happened to Me!"

Sometimes, the topic of a conversation seems to invite you to share your own, similar experiences. For example, someone is excitedly telling you about their first business trip to Hong Kong. This immediately triggers memories of your own experiences in Hong Kong, both for work and for pleasure. Rather than appreciating the speaker's experiences, you are mentally reminiscing and preparing to offer your own carefully chosen anecdote—that time that you scheduled a business meeting in a dim sum restaurant where the waiting staff interrupted every couple of minutes to offer you some delicious delicacies. We call this *comparing*. Of course, there is nothing inherently wrong with comparing. Potentially, it can create bonding through a sense of shared experience.

But the point is that you are ignoring the speaker's needs. What is it they are implicitly asking for in the conversation? It might be admiration from you, an acknowledgment of their enthusiasm, or a bit of respect for their work.

2. Competing: "That's Nothing—I Have Had It Much Tougher Than That!"

There is a joke about three people competing to outdo one another with how difficult things were during their childhoods. The first person says, "I was so poor that I had to sleep in a tent on the sidewalk." The second chimes in, saying "You had a tent? All I had was a piece of cardboard!" Not to be outdone, the third person says "Cardboard? I would have loved to have some cardboard to protect myself from the rain."

People are social creatures and it is common for friends and colleagues to share challenges they are experiencing. An office mate might say "I'm really struggling to get through my emails! I have over 200 unread emails sitting in my inbox!" It is easy to assume that they are looking for some sympathy or perhaps some ideas for dealing with the overwhelm. Instead of offering either of these, however, you respond, "Just 200? I have over 1,000 emails that I need to respond to!" We call this *competing*. Again, there is nothing wrong with sharing your own experience, but it runs the risk of appearing unsympathetic, self-absorbed, or checked-out.

3. Mind Reading: "I Know What You're Going to Say."

By the time each of us reaches adulthood, we have accumulated a vast web of knowledge and a storehouse of personal experiences. Although this helps us understand how to interact at a takeaway restaurant or share ideas at a planning meeting, it can also get in the way of effective listening. Take a moment to consider this question: Can you think of any recent interactions in which you were pretty sure what was going to happen even *before* the conversation took place? This is called *mind reading*.

One of us had to share news of a merger—a larger organization was buying the smaller one. At the first meeting, we made the mistake of assuming that everyone would be very concerned and anxious. Instead of going in with a positive slant, the presentation was defensive and targeted at people who would resist the change. This bias—even if it was rooted in experience—interfered with our ability to engage positively with the team. Mind reading runs the risk of focusing on your own assumptions rather than the views and interests of others. Unless you are actually a mind reader, believing that you know what other people will say becomes a barrier to genuinely listening.

4. Unsolicited Advice: "If I Were in Your Shoes..."

A leader of a team in another department confides in you how difficult it is for them to take a vacation and totally unplug from work. When people come to us to talk about problems they face, it is easy for us to go straight to problem-solving mode. This can lead to responses ranging from the unhelpful ("you should just trust your team while you are away") to the microscopic ("you should create a special alert on your phone that is only to be used in emergencies").

This is an instance that calls for optimal support matching. Rather than breaking out the toolbox, it is wiser to listen to what is being asked for. It might be that your colleague would appreciate some suggestions. Or, it may be that they just want someone to commiserate with them. Whatever the case, one thing is certain: If you are busy giving unsolicited advice—attempting to solve another person's problem—while they are talking to you, then you are not listening.

5. Priority Status: "I Know Best."

Imagine you are in a work meeting, and people are discussing a technical issue that is in your area of expertise. You have had years of experience resolving technical issues just like the one being discussed! You might be inclined to think, "I know so much more about this than everyone here." Or, imagine that you are watching a junior colleague make their first pitch; something you have done dozens of times. In both cases, you recognize—accurately—that you have knowledge and experience relevant to the situation. The problem— where listening is concerned—is that it is easy to believe that this expertise should give you priority. We call this *priority status* and it occurs when people quit listening and, instead, rush to share their own ideas. To be certain, people typically share their own perspectives out of a desire to help. Although there may be some merit in doing so, it is still the case that your enthusiasm to share your own ideas is likely to mean that you will have stopped listening to the conversation.

6. Time Poverty: "I Don't Have Time for This."

Personal hygiene, grocery shopping, commuting, childcare, meal preparation, seeing friends, exercise, email, laundry, holiday decorating. Our personal lives are so packed with activity that it hardly seems possible that there is time for our regular jobs. Our work, in turn, is also overfull with meetings, calls, writing, and countless other schedule-bursting activities. Unfortunately, there are still only twenty-four hours in a day, so there is a tendency to feel like time is always in short supply. This so-called *time poverty* can interfere with our concentration and focus. In our minds, we are saying to the other person, "Come on, hurry up, we don't have time for this." In these situations, we can come across as impatient or appear to have made a judgment about the significance of what they are saying. This impatience will make people feel that you do not value what they have to say and that you are not listening.

There are more than six mental barriers to listening but these are among the most common. To verify this, just have a look at responses to social media posts. You may recognize quite a few of the barriers mentioned here! Noticing these internal barriers when they occur is, perhaps, the first step in mitigating them (see Table 2.2). It may also be helpful to identify mental barriers that interfere with your personal listening. These might include experiencing acute stress in your own life, feeling you do not understand the speaker's cultural context, fearing that you might come across as ignorant, being uninterested in the

TABLE 2.2 Mitigating obstacles to listening

Obstacle	Mitigation strategies
Comparing	• Remind yourself to be more interested in their experience than sharing your own. • Get curious about their situation and ask for more information.
Competing	• Remember the intention of the conversation and acknowledge the other person's experiences. • Save your own anecdotes for a future conversation.
Mind reading	• Acknowledge that you cannot be sure about what will happen. • Adopt a more open mind, giving others the benefit of the doubt.
Unsolicited advice	• Check whether there has been an explicit request for advice, suggestions, or solutions. • Turn your attention to listening and being empathetic.
Priority status	• Be part of the conversation by listening to other people's experiences. • Offer to share your own experiences tentatively after allowing others to speak.
Time poverty	• Consider how important it is to be respectful to the other person. • If appropriate, signal how much time is available for the conversation.

topic of conversation, or many other factors. Gaining self-awareness about your own unique biases will help you to better recognize when you are not listening and to tailor your mitigation strategies.

GETTING IT WRONG, PART TWO: ANTI-SOCIAL LISTENING

The other class of obstacles to great listening is what we call "antisocial listening." As the name suggests, the intention of this type of listening is not to connect with another person or understand them. Instead, it is a series of motives that are fundamentally self-serving. It is a form of listening that places the emphasis on you—the listener—rather than on the speaker. As with the internal obstacles, there are likely dozens of antisocial motives. Here, we focus on five of the most common.

1. Listening to Inform

Have you ever asked the question "Do you understand?" just so that you can explain things in more detail? If so, your intention was likely more about your opportunity to offer information than it was to check on another person's comprehension. Listening to inform is common, in part, because it feels good. It can boost our self-esteem to demonstrate our knowledge, and it can leave us feeling helpful to others, even when the reality is that our explanations are unnecessary.

2. Listening to Brag

Have you ever asked a pointed question about a person's holiday (such as inquiring if they visited a particular island or beach—one that you have visited—on their recent trip to Thailand)? If so, perhaps your intention was not to find out about the other person's experiences but to create the conditions for sharing your own? By asking a question about the other person's experience, you guided the conversation in a direction that allowed you an opportunity to share your own experience. One of the reasons that this obstacle is so pervasive is that listeners easily convince themselves that it leads to a better connection. If we both had a nice time while visiting the island of Koh Phi Phi, the logic goes, then that is a point of commonality. Unfortunately, sharing your own experience is often a less effective strategy for connecting than simply listening and appreciating what others are telling you.

3. Listening to Defend

Have you ever asked, "Why do you say that?" just so that you could formulate counter-arguments to each point? If so, your intention was not to understand another person's point of view but to defend your own. Every one of us is occasionally guilty of this approach to listening. You know what it feels like. In your head you are creating lists of rebuttals. It feels like having a support team in your head reassuring you that you are right and that the speaker is wrong. What it does not feel like is listening.

4. Listening to Find Fault

Have you ever listened to a presentation or report with a specific focus on whether the speaker makes any mistakes or errors? If so, you were listening to critique rather than listening to learn. As with some of the other antisocial approaches to listening, we can convince ourselves that listening to find fault is helpful. Is it not better that a person knows where the holes and problems lie? The problem with this approach links back to optimal support matching. It may not, in fact, be what the speaker is asking for. Unless there is an explicit request for critical feedback, listening to find fault is not really listening at all.

5. Listening to Undermine

Have you ever gone into a conversation determined *not* to listen? If so, you might have entered the interaction hoping to undermine the speaker. This sounds dramatic but is surprisingly common. People disagree over policies, procedures, and politics. In each of these cases, a listener can be disinclined to actually listen. Instead, they are hoping to marshal their own views to persuade an audience, offer an alternative, or discredit an argument that they find objectionable. Approaching a conversation in this way might lead to you scoring some points but it rarely leads to mutual understanding or appreciation.

GETTING IT RIGHT: THE TWO INTENTIONAL MODES OF RADICAL LISTENING

So far, it might sound as if the news around intentional listening is bleak. Life is too busy. The world is too full of distractions. People harbor too many selfish motives. We are too often the victims of natural psychological biases to listen effectively. Taken together, this might leave you scratching your head and wondering how we ever hear a word another person says. The good news is that there is good news. Most of the listening obstacles we have described occur when we are on autopilot. When we are more intentional about our listening, we can elevate our conversations. The first step of becoming more intentional as a listener is to distinguish between "listening for" and "listening (in order) to."

"Listening For"

We have asked therapists, executive coaches, and visionary leaders about their listening habits. When we ask great listeners how they listen, the most common responses focus on what they are *listening for*. "Listening for" is the idea that you can keep an ear out for something specific. Some of our interviewees talked about listening for emotional tone. One person said: "I pay particular attention to how people are feeling. I consider which emotions I can pick up from someone's voice or posture." Another person told us that they consistently keep an ear out for what is conspicuously absent in a discussion: "I like to notice what the other person is *not* saying. What are they leaving out? Is there something they are avoiding?"

A common thread among people who listen well was paying attention to the speaker's motivation. In some cases, they reported that listening is about understanding what motivates the speaker; having an appreciation of their values and enthusiasm. In other instances, listeners honed in on understanding the motive for the conversation; seeking clarity about why the person was raising an issue and what they were hoping to accomplish by doing so.

Whether the intention was to listen for strengths, hidden agendas, original ideas, gossip, alignment, or excitement, great listeners tend to focus on a reliable set of attention targets (see Table 2.3).

The sheer number of targets we can keep an ear out for is one of the reasons why great listening is not ubiquitous. It can be challenging to pick up on linguistic cues while simultaneously trying to understand the basic message being conveyed as well as the motives

TABLE 2.3 Listening for

Listening for . . .	Examples
Themes	Concepts—perhaps unspoken—that connect or summarize what is being said, such as "independence" or "trust" or "self-doubt"
Emotion	Tone of voice, emotional expressions, potential mismatch between what is verbally and visually expressed, feelings that arise in the listener
Language	Word choice, pace of speech, inflection and emphasis, use of metaphor, repeated phrases
Content	The basic message being conveyed, the clarity of that message, the context in which the discussion is happening

behind it. In fact, trying to keep all these targets in mind can distract from listening well! This is where intentionality comes in. If you understand what you are trying to accomplish in your listening, then you can focus your attention on just the most relevant and important of these cues. This is where "listening (in order) to" becomes a useful companion to "listening for."

"Listening (In Order) To"

At the core of the Radical Listening skill of intention is the concept of *listening (in order) to*. This is one way that Radical Listening differs from traditional active listening. Where the latter focuses on comprehension, the former emphasizes the intention for listening. By this, we mean that listening is undertaken with the intention to accomplish a specific objective. You can identify your intention before a single word has been spoken. In other words, knowing your *primary motivation* before the start of a conversation increases the chances that it will be beneficial for you and the people you will be listening to. As the term implies, it is helpful to know the *main* reason for listening to someone. There are many possible motivations for listening but six of them are more common (see Table 2.4). What is more, these six can be placed into two relatively distinct categories: social motivations (having to do with relationships) and cognitive motivations (having to do with thinking).

SOCIAL MOTIVATIONS

To Connect

This is the intention to build a strong social connection with another person or a group of people. This is the type of motivated listening in which you engage when you first meet someone you really like and want to learn about them. When your intention is to connect, it tends

TABLE 2.4 Listening in order to

Listening in order to . . .	Trends in the focus of your attention
Connect	Commonalities, admirable qualities
Appreciate	Another person's point of view, experience, or efforts
Influence	Another person's motivation, values, strength of conviction
Understand	Away from critique, toward an openness to key concepts
Solve	Technical or practical details, causes, processes
Learn	Novel or confusing ideas or concepts, concepts that link to preexisting knowledge

to focus your attention on the positive aspects of the speaker or their message. You are more likely to notice, for example, shared experiences, mutual interests, or admirable qualities of the speaker. Moreover, when you are interested in connecting you are more likely to listen well, giving them more space to speak and asking more curious questions. This motivation can demonstrate to people that you are invested in them.

To Appreciate

This is the intention to acknowledge or validate another person's contributions, way of being, or efforts. When you are driven by this motive, you are more likely to focus on the role the speaker has played in the events they are describing. This type of listening activates your empathy; engaging you in the task of appreciating, to the extent possible, the other person's point of view. Listening to appreciate also demonstrates to others that you value their input.

To Influence

This is the intention to encourage people to feel or think in a particular way. It can be counterintuitive to think of listening as a persuasive tool because we most often think of persuasion as having to do with speech, such as making a pitch or offering an argument. As an example, it is possible to listen in a way that builds a person's self-esteem, increases their motivation, or encourages them to be more open to feedback. Listening in this way allows you to positively influence those around you.

COGNITIVE MOTIVATIONS

To Understand

This is likely the most common intention for listening and the most common understanding of what listening is. To put it simply, people listen in order to understand the views, positions, or situations of others. Listening in this way helps you veer away from critique or other distractions and focus wholeheartedly on comprehension.

To Solve

This is a very specific type of listening. Here, the intention of listening is to gather sufficient information to support others to solve problems or overcome barriers. This form of listening can be highly technical and expert, as in the case of a doctor listening to a list of symptoms in order to make an accurate diagnosis. It can also focus you on personal experience and accumulated life wisdom, as in the case of offering advice to a newly promoted colleague. Listening in this way equips you to be a good thought partner in problem-solving conversations.

To Learn

This is the intention to take in as much information as possible and add it to your existing web of knowledge. This is the mode of listening that is most often associated with being a student but it is just as relevant to work or other areas of life. Listening in this way focuses your attention on novel or interesting ideas, concepts that align with preexisting knowledge, or messages that run counter to what you know. Listening in this way tends to demonstrate your curiosity to others.

SUMMARY

Listening is more than simply hearing or understanding. We argue that it begins with setting a clear intention for what you want to accomplish by listening and being clear on what, specifically, you are keeping an ear out for. In some ways, you can think of intentionality as part of a *pre-listening* ritual. Radical Listening recasts listening as a proactive social process rather than a reactive one. Being clear about your purpose before an interaction not only allows you to accomplish a personal or professional goal but will also motivate you to listen in a way that is most helpful for your conversational partner.

QUESTIONS

1. What is your most common intention in listening?
2. Which obstacles are most familiar to you?
3. How does the concept of "optimal support matching" affect the way you think about your listening?

PART TWO

INTERNAL LISTENING SKILLS

Listening is, largely, an internal phenomenon. When we speak to others, the process of listening and taking in information happens somewhere within us. In the following three chapters, we will discuss the internal skills of listening. We will begin with *noticing*. Our intention heavily influences what we pay attention to and notice in a conversation. This includes many dimensions of communication such as emotional expression, pace, tone, and language, among others. Next, we cover the skill of *quiet*. Quiet is the foundation of great listening. Here we focus on more than just "remaining quiet." Instead, we talk about the uses of silence in conversation, the role of pauses, and cross-cultural differences in the understanding of silence. This section concludes with a chapter on the skill of *acceptance*. It is important not to conflate accepting what people say with agreeing with them. We propose that acceptance is a willingness to consider ideas, rather than an imperative to endorse them. We will conclude by proposing two mental orientations to conversation—intellectual humility and curiosity—that can enable us to be more accepting.

CHAPTER THREE

NOTICING

In 2017, the Institute for Research in Schools (IRIS) provided data from the International Space Station to students across the United Kingdom. The mission of IRIS is to engage students in science, technology, and math by providing real data sets for them to analyze. The 2017 data was a record of the radiation levels being documented by the space station. Students across the United Kingdom were looking at spreadsheets to learn more about measurement and analysis.

One student noticed something that no one else did. Miles Soloman, a 17-year-old from Sheffield, saw that some of the energy being recorded was listed with a value of negative one.[1] Miles noticed that this problematic reading seemed to be occurring multiple times a day. Because negative energy is an impossibility, Miles and his teacher contacted NASA. The space agency, in turn, was highly appreciative and corrected the error in their computer algorithm.

Miles's case illustrates some important lessons about noticing. First, looking is not the same thing as noticing. Hundreds of people had been poring over the same numbers as Miles but they either failed to see the anomaly, or if they did, they simply explained it away. Second, noticing is a special instance of intentionally focusing one's attention. In Miles's case, he was curious about the smallest measures of energy and so directed his attention to just this portion of the massive spreadsheet which led him to spot the impossible negative numbers.

Many of us are not as mathematically gifted or analytically savvy as Miles, but it is still easy to see the ways that noticing happens—or does not—in our daily lives. "Where is the tomato ketchup?" we ask as we stand in front of the open door of a refrigerator, even though a bottle of ketchup is in the door, right next to us. We might see the cashier at the supermarket having a coffee in the local cafe and not make the connection. We drive to the office instead of dropping the kids at school because the route to work is habitual. We are more likely to notice the same make and model of car as the one we drive. We fail to notice small errors in films, such as an actor's shirt being buttoned and then unbuttoned and then buttoned again in a single scene. We are more likely to notice our colleagues at work but less likely to notice who is out sick.

UNDERSTANDING ATTENTION

To understand the concept of noticing, we need to explore how attention works. The ideas are so closely related that it can be difficult to disentangle noticing from attention. After all, if you *notice* that it is noon it makes sense to think that this is because you are *paying attention* to the time. It turns out that there are subtle differences between these two processes. A rule of thumb for distinguishing noticing from attention is that noticing is typically more conscious than attention. Even so, they are best thought of as gears that turn together. In this chapter, we will provide a basic overview of attention and then link it to the skill of noticing. It is our hope that by better understanding the mechanics of attention, you will be able to improve the way that you notice.

We all have an intuitive grasp of what attention is. After all, we use it every day. Defining the concept of attention, however, is not easy to do with any precision. The *Oxford Dictionary of Psychology* states that attention is "sustained concentration on a specific stimulus, sensation, idea, thought, or activity."[2] The word concentration suggests that attention is largely (but, perhaps, not wholly) an intentional phenomenon. In fact, the limits of conscious attention are an endless source of research fascination. The word "sustained" in the definition suggests that it requires effort and intention. No wonder we use the phrase "to pay attention."

The phrase "pay attention" first appeared in written English in the 1700s, most notably in court documents.[3] Today, we use the phrase so commonly that it is hard to think of an alternative. What did they say about attention before the year 1700? One answer can be found in the works of Shakespeare. In the play Henry IV, Part 1, for example, Falstaff admits to being a poor listener. He describes himself as having "the disease of not listening, the malady of not marking."[4]

Today, by contrast, we add verbs to the word attention to make it sound like one of the most fun and dynamic of psychological states. You can attract attention, call attention to, come to attention, snap to attention, draw attention to, hold someone's attention, be hungry for attention (even starving for attention), have a short attention span, direct attention, and—of course—pay attention. We see the solitary word "attention," followed by an exclamation point and issued as a command on prescription pill bottles, email headers, signs warning of a wet floor, and people issuing an emergency announcement.

WHAT THE RESEARCH SAYS

You would think that with all the use our attention gets, we would be pretty good at it. In the modern era, however, there is increasing concern about the ways that technology—to name just a single influence—is interfering with our ability to "pay attention." Some highly publicized surveys suggest that humans have a shorter attention span than a goldfish![5] That might not be so bad if goldfish had amazing attention, but reports estimate that they can focus for about nine seconds. Many scholars of attention have criticized these eye-popping statistics by pointing out the fact that they are not based on research published in respected, peer reviewed journals.

Despite the lack of systematic evidence, this kind of reporting about attention generates cocktail party buzz and society acts accordingly. A few decades ago, for example, television advertisements were commonly thirty seconds to a minute in length. In the age of smartphones, advertisements are often as short as six seconds. Anyone who has waited for a fifteen-second advert to run before their preferred video loads knows that a quarter of a minute can seem like a long time. Even shots in movies have decreased over time and now each shot is about four seconds long. Further, people now have the ability—and desire—to speed up audiobooks and podcasts from real-time speeds to one and a quarter or one and a half times faster. Even newspapers are reducing the length of articles with fewer opting for long-form journalism. This might be a chicken-and-egg problem: are content creators shortening content because they believe people cannot pay attention or are they artificially shortening our collective attention with their bite-sized content?

Another reason people are ready to accept dwindling attention spans is because of related phenomena. For example, there is a rise in the diagnosis of ADHD, but this could be because we are better able to identify it than we have been in the past or because we overdiagnose it. Similarly, many people feel that their attention is getting shorter because, anecdotally, they find themselves checking their phones when they experience even a few seconds of boredom. This is a logical fallacy which overlooks the idea that before we all had smartphones, we likely turned to doodling, chores, looking out the window, or day-dreaming when we experienced micro-boredom.

What does the academic research on the topic say? Among the leading authorities on the impact of media technology on attention is Dr. Gloria Mark, at the University of California. Mark and her research team were interested in tracking attention while people worked on their screens.[6] They wanted to know how long a person would stick to a single task, such as writing in a Word document, before jumping to a distinct task, such as checking email. Over a span of years, they used stopwatches and computer logs to track people's ability to concentrate. They discovered a steady decline over time (see Figure 3.1) from about two and a half minutes at the beginning of the 2000s to

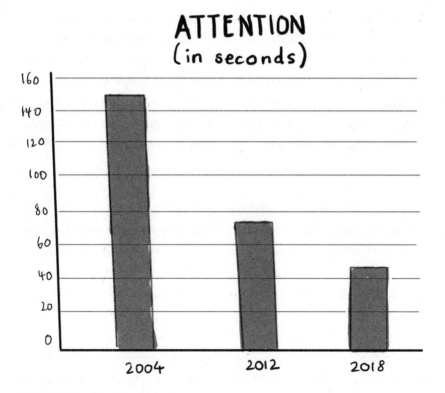

FIGURE 3.1 Declining attention spans

an average of forty-seven seconds during the period just before the COVID-19 pandemic.

Dr. Mark is quick to caution that these findings do not represent some type of attentional apocalypse. Whereas people seem less focused on some digital work tasks it is easy to see the ways in which people easily focus on inherently enjoyable tasks, spending hours concentrating on hobbies such as painting or gardening, being able to have long conversations with friends, and even being able to focus on electronic media such as video games and movies.

HARNESSING OUR ATTENTION

What, then, are we to make of all this competing information? Although there is not strong evidence that the innate capacity to concentrate has decreased there are certainly more distractions, especially online, than there have been in the past. Perhaps the question is not whether people's attention spans are shrinking but, instead, what are the ways that we maintain or lose focus throughout the day. To understand this, it is helpful to think of attention not as a general focus but in terms of specific types of attention.

Divided Attention

There are many types of attention. Perhaps the one that is the most problematic is divided attention.[7] Divided attention is what happens when we multitask. Eating a sandwich while reading the news. Having a conversation while checking text messages. Writing an email to a customer while mentally replaying an argument with a colleague. Driving to work while thinking about a grocery list. Working on a team project while the office loudly celebrates someone's birthday just outside the conference room door. As you might expect, when you do not give your full attention to something, you notice less about it, remember less about it, and—in the case of a task—perform it less well.

The classic illustration of this can be found in what researchers call the "Stroop task," named after psychologist John Stroop. An early pioneer of research on mental processing, Stroop created a clever method for befuddling his study participants. The task involves saying the color that a word is written in. For example, if you read the word "stakeholder" and it is written in blue font, you would say "blue." This appears easy enough until you must read a word that is, itself, the name of a color. In this example, imagine reading the word "blue" but it is written in purple ink. The word and the color it is written in provide competing information. What happens in this case is that people take longer to sift through the information to come up with the correct answer ("purple").

A similar thing happens when we engage in so-called task switching: jumping rapidly from one task to another.[8] For example, when you listen to a colleague who stops by your desk to update you about an upcoming business trip while you are sending a text to another colleague. Although this is divided attention, it is also task switching because you are jumping back and forth between listening and writing. Task switching has mental costs because there is slippage as you shift from one mode of thinking to another. The costs vary but, in general, they are the types of things you would expect: lower levels of memory and recall, poorer execution of a task, confusion, and inefficiency.

The good news about the related problems of divided attention and task switching is that there is a clear solution: do less of it. There is a long list of straightforward strategies that can help you stay focused:

• *Prioritization.* Having a clearly articulated priority list can help you focus. There can be an emotional reward in starting the workday by opening your email—after all, it is full of novelty—but it is typically not the smartest way to allocate your attention. What's more, if you find yourself jumping to low-priority tasks, you have clearly strayed from your plan. When this happens, it is a signal to take a quick break and an opportunity to redouble your focus on what is important.

• *Strategic interruption.* Coworkers knock on your door with a "quick question," you get a Slack message every five minutes, you get a phone call, or your supervisor wants to give you feedback. Each of these represents some mental slippage as you try to reorient yourself to the flow of work. As an alternative to these disruptions, you can block out time when interruption is off-limits and schedule time when it is acceptable.

• *Remove smartphones and similar distractions.* Smartphones are amazing devices but they are also a major source of distraction. In a study of hundreds of South Korean nursing students, nearly half used their phones for nonwork reasons during their clinical practice.[9] In another study, Chinese professionals reported using their mobile phones to check the time, check text messages, send texts, and check emails all while participating in work meetings.[10] What is more, they were more likely to do this when meeting with their coworkers than with visitors or supervisors. A host of other studies reveal that when there is a smartphone present, it interferes with social interaction[11] and people's feelings of interpersonal enjoyment diminish.[12] This does not mean that you have to throw your phone in the ocean; it simply suggests that you can create simple new habits such as keeping it in a drawer instead of on your desk or leaving it in your office when you go to a meeting.

Selective Attention

Perhaps the most common type of attention is "selective attention."[13] This is when a person concentrates on something specific while ignoring other things. When you read a report and focus on the cost and revenue numbers but overlook the font size and page numbers, that is selective attention. Trying to figure out a person's motivation by listening to their word choice and analyzing their posture and facial expression is also selective attention. Selective attention acts like a spotlight, with the beam concentrated on one point and everything else cloaked in attentional darkness.

Selective attention is a useful tool. Without too much mental effort, we can filter out potentially distracting information. You rarely notice the sound of an airplane flying overhead and you can quickly ignore the noise of a nearby phone conversation if you are trying to focus on an important task. Without selective attention we would be victims to every sight, sound, and smell in our environments. We would be overwhelmed by the sound of turning pages, the squeak of office chairs, the hum of lights, the murmur of background conversations, the robotic scanning of copy machines, the patter of footsteps, the venting of air conditioners, the squishing sound of chewing, the ringing of phones, the thud of closing doors, the sudden barks of laughter, and the guttural clearing of throats. There is a tidal wave of sound that we can block out in favor of what we deem to be important.

Even when we are listening selectively, however, our subconscious is scanning the horizon for potentially interesting or important information. This is why you notice the electronic ping of digital messages and why you perk up at the sound of an ambulance but then dismiss it if it is not relevant to you. This also explains the so-called "cocktail party effect." This effect happens when you catch the sound of your name being spoken across a room in another conversation. The effect is not limited to your name, either. You are more likely to suddenly pick up on distant mentions of keywords that are relevant to you: the name of the town you were raised in, the name of the company at which you work, the name of your sister, or the name of the book you are currently reading.

When it comes to attention and listening, we know a great deal about how it works from so-called "dichotic listening" studies. Using headphones, researchers feed two separate messages, one into each of a listener's ears. For example, you might have the audiobook of Harry Potter piped into your right ear while the daily news is coming into your left. Your task would be to "shadow" or repeat what is being said in your left ear. People are generally pretty good at this, because of selective attention.

Here, we arrive at the potential downside of selective attention. When a person pays special attention to one thing, they miss noticing other things. In dichotic listening studies, people are unable to report on the content of the blocked message. For example, in one classic dichotic listening study the message changed from English to German and the research participants were unaware because they were focusing on a different message.[14] Here is an even more surprising result.

A list of simple words was presented in one ear while research participants were asked to "shadow" (or repeat) a passage that was presented in the other ear. The word list was repeated thirty-five times but participants were unable to recall any of the words.[15] What is more, a follow-up study used the participants' names, giving them instructions like "John Smith, you can stop now" or "John Smith, change to the other ear." Even in these cases, people only heard the blocked message half of the time. This suggests that when we focus intently, we miss just about everything else.

This phenomenon is known as "inattentional blindness." A name so jargony that you probably will not be repeating it to friends and colleagues unless you are trying to show off. In simple terms, it is the failure to notice something that ought to be obvious because attention is directed elsewhere. Psychologists love to demonstrate this effect precisely because it can be so dramatic. In the 1970s, researchers had two teams of people pass balls.[16] One team wore white shirts and the other team wore black shirts. Research participants were instructed to count the number of passes from the white team but to ignore those from the team in black. Then, a woman in a raincoat, holding an umbrella, walked through the middle of the game. The participants were so focused on their counting task that they largely failed to notice the interloper. Later, researchers recreated this experiment; this time having a person dressed in a gorilla suit walk through the game. About 50 percent of people missed this startling and obvious intrusion, giving rise to the term "the invisible gorilla" which is a fine alternative to "inattentional blindness."

The invisible gorilla phenomenon is more than just a psychology party trick. It has real-world implications. Consider the findings of research on flight simulators that use a head-up display to project altitude and airspeed onto the pilot's windshield. It turns out that when researchers place unexpected objects in the pilot's view, such as another plane blocking the runway, the pilots often miss this information.[17] Or consider the research in which radiologists were asked to look at X-rays of lungs to identify potential signs of cancer. Researchers placed an image of an angry gorilla on the slides and a whopping 83 percent of the doctors missed it because they were so focused on looking for one particular type of nodule in the X-ray.[18] In the case of both the pilots and the oncologists, shining the spotlight of attention one place left another place dark.

When it comes to listening—whether it is hearing a colleague's complaint, listening to the direction of a supervisor, or attending an all-staff meeting—knowing that you will not and cannot notice all the information can be helpful. It is a clear reminder that just showing up and keeping your ears open is not enough. Instead, you need to be intentional about what you want to pay attention to. What would be the most important things to notice? Emotional expressions that might suggest a person's motives or buy-in? Numbers in a chart that could be used to persuade a customer? The details of a project deadline so that you can plan accordingly? By entering the meeting intentionally, you can budget your attention, spending it where it will be most useful.

Shared Attention

Shared attention is a unique form of attention. It occurs when two or more people focus on the same thing. Examples include when an audience enjoys a ballet performance, a family watches television, students listen to a lecture, and a team attends a presentation on a proposed product launch. Shared attention, it turns out, confers several benefits above and beyond a person's individual attention. In one study, people were given lists of words to memorize. When they believed that their list was the same as that of another research participant, they were better at accurately recalling the words.[19] That is right; the belief that another person was putting in effort on the same list of words improved performance.

It is tempting to think that this is the result of competition—and that may be a factor for some highly competitive people—but that is not the best explanation. People who pay attention together are more likely to feel a greater sense of camaraderie ("we are doing this"), feel a greater sense of importance ("what we are paying attention to must be worth paying attention to because we are all doing it"), and experience enhanced motivation ("if it is worth paying attention to, we should put some effort into it").

In an era in which work meetings have frequently moved online and smartphones vie for attention, shared attention is an important topic. Over a meeting platform like Zoom or Microsoft Teams, there is a reduced sense of shared attention. Each attendee might have a different view enabled and each might be looking at a different person. What is more, each person—calling in from home or an office—is in a unique context and will be seeing and hearing elements that are unique to them, such as the ringing of a doorbell, the sound of a pet wanting out, or the chatting of nearby people. The downside risk is that in these environments the mild drop in shared attention will lead to lesser feelings of connection, importance, and motivation.

It is not all doom and gloom, however. According to Dr. Beth Morling, a psychologist at the University of Delaware, shared attention is part of a larger human need to share our inner states.[20] This behavior starts when people are very young. If a caregiving adult turns and looks at something, for instance, an eight-month-old baby will follow their gaze to see what it is. Similarly, babies around that same age start pointing at objects such as a toy or bottle in the hope that adults will notice those things as well. According to Morling, shared attention is one aspect of a larger phenomenon called "shared reality."

Shared reality is what we call those quirky moments where it almost seems as if two people share a mind. When you say, "I was just going to say the exact same thing!" you have experienced shared reality with another person. When two people seem to completely agree on an opinion, when one person feels deeply listened to and understood, when people are startled at the same time, these are all examples of shared reality.

In the same vein, Radical Listening is a shared experience. It does not mean that the conversational partners will have the same opinions, the same attitudes, or the same thoughts. It does, however, mean that they will feel connected because they will be so wholly immersed in the same moment. The speaker will feel validated by the listener's demonstration of attention. That is, it is not enough to pay attention; you must *demonstrate* that you are paying attention. One of the best ways to do that is by noticing things that are important to your conversational partner.

NOTICING AND THE ACT OF RADICAL LISTENING

Imagine that you get the juggling act of attention just right. You remove or ignore distractions to cut down on divided attention.

You harness your selective attention, pointing it toward the speaker you are listening to. You are aware of the shared attention between you. You have prepped the ground of listening, making it fertile for the sowing of noticing. Great listening is largely about what you notice.

When someone speaks to you, certain things stand out. If they have a piece of food stuck in their teeth, or are wearing a huge piece of jewelry, or if they use a word with which you are unfamiliar, or if they stand too close for comfort, or if they repeat themselves, or if they speak with an accent, or if they choose their words carefully. The list goes on and on. These types of things call your attention because they are distinctive in some way.

It is tempting to think of this noticing as synonymous with mindfulness. As in, "If I simply pay attention, I will notice more details." Although this is certainly true, it is also not the whole story. What we notice, it turns out, is heavily influenced by our intention. If our intention is to entertain, for instance, we might be more likely to notice funny words, logical inconsistencies, or pauses in which we can insert a humorous comment. We are, in essence, ready to spring; to jump into the conversation, and we are specifically looking for opportunities to do so. By contrast, if our intention is to understand another person, we are more likely to remain silent and pay attention to their emotional expressions and nonverbal cues.

Noticing and intention sit comfortably with one another. Together, they answer the question, "What am I paying attention to?" People from different work roles listen differently. That is, they try to notice unique aspects of conversation. People in the justice system—detectives and prosecuting attorneys, say—pay attention to the story that is being told about a crime. They are trying to notice inconsistencies that might suggest that the speaker is lying or withholding information. A manager, by contrast, might be listening in order to notice the emotional language with which a team describes their work. In this case, the manager tries to gauge team morale and listens carefully for complaints or positivity.

Understanding what you are listening for—where to focus the beam of your attention—is the critical step in noticing useful information in a conversation. We can divide noticing into various general categories (shown in Table 3.1). These categories can serve as multiple channels of information.

When it comes to noticing language itself—the words, sentences, and stories that people tell us—it is possible to create categories to help guide our attention. These include what a person says, how they say it, and why they say it (see Table 3.2). Bearing in mind that what is said—the actual words used—is just the tip of the linguistic iceberg. The style in which it is said and the rationale behind the words are, arguably, more important.

Paying attention to a person's style of speech can be a source of a great deal of information. Doing this comes naturally, in certain instances. When a person speaks your language with a slight accent, for instance, you can guess that it is likely that they learned it as a second language or may have grown up in a society with a different dialect.

TABLE 3.1 General categories of noticing

Level of noticing	Definition	Examples
Physical	The speaker's posture, dress, facial expressions, and gestures	Smiling, slumping over, looking away, wearing a suit
Behavioral	The speaker's actions	Crying, checking text messages, smashing a fist on a desk
Mental	Language and word choice that suggests the speaker's emotional state, values, attitudes, motives, or goals	"I'm confused" "I'm opposed to moving forward on this"
Social	Language or stories that provide insight about the nature of the speaker's relationships	"The team seems content to let me do all the work when it comes to presenting"

TABLE 3.2 What, how, and why

	Definition	Example
What is said	These are the actual words regardless of how they are intended or interpreted	"I would never mislead our investors"
How it is said	This is the style in which it is said and includes attention to jargon, absolute statements	"*I* would never mislead our investors" (with an emphasis on "I")
Why it is said	This is the listener's hypothesis about the values and motives that underlie the statement	"*I* would never mislead our investors" (said by a defendant in a court-room)

When a person uses jargon with which you are familiar, it can be a nod to their perception of you as a "knowledge insider." On the other hand, if they use jargon that is unfamiliar to you it could be an indication that they do not understand your background well or that they are so ensconced in their field that they forget how to interact with "knowledge outsiders." The language becomes exclusionary instead of inclusive.

One of the most obvious, and important, aspects of style of speech is emotional tone. If a colleague asks "Why did you do that?" in a harsh tone, it comes across as accusatory. If they ask the same question with eyebrows raised and a light emotional tone it comes across as curious. A speaker's emotional tone gives clues to how they see a situation and to what they are trying to accomplish.

SUMMARY

Human attention is a filter. We are not sponges absorbing 100 percent of the sights and sounds around us. Instead, we selectively take in, notice, and use bits of information here and there. Our attention is like a spotlight and, if we are intentional, we can shine it on the details that matter most.

QUESTIONS

1. What are the biggest distractors of your attention when interacting with others? What might you do to mitigate these?

2. What are your attitudes and habits regarding multitasking? How does learning about the science of attention impact these beliefs?

3. It is easy to say that you are paying attention to someone who is speaking. What, specifically, can you do to *demonstrate* that attention to them?

CHAPTER FOUR

QUIET

Around the world, people seem to be of two minds about the concept of quiet. On the one hand, people appear to value quietness. In our societies, we have created spaces that insist on it, such as libraries, houses of worship, and cemeteries. Theaters and cinemas ask people to quiet their electronic devices before the show starts. Teachers admonish their students to keep quiet so that they can listen to lessons and, presumably, learn more in the process. Movie directors yell "Quiet on the set" to ensure that only the most important sounds are captured. Hunters remain as silent as possible to avoid scaring potential prey and to better hear it approaching. People even pay to go on silent retreats or take holidays away from the bustle—noise—of urban environments. We say "silence is a virtue." People seem to have an intuitive understanding that quiet forms a foundation upon which good listening can be built. We assume that we can hear better when we are enveloped in quiet.

On the other hand, quiet—and especially its more extreme cousin, silence—sometimes has a bad reputation. To stay silent in the face of flagrant injustice, for example, is seen as shameful. Similarly, when someone is "too quiet" we worry that something might be wrong with them. When people are silent, they are often assumed to be passive, and their opinions are often ignored. When our partners dish out the "silent treatment," it is a punishment rather than a pleasant, calming experience. Apart from some film buffs, we would rather see modern movies than old-time silent ones. During a comedy routine, complete silence in the audience would suggest that the comedian is having a bad night. In Chinese culture, people prize the hustle and bustle of a loud restaurant. They even have a word—*rènao*—that literally means "hot noise" and is perceived as exciting and lively. And, just as people pay to vacation on peaceful, secluded beaches, they also pay to attend sports events, rock concerts, and other raucous activities. In these examples, we can see evidence that people are, at times, uncomfortable with silence.

How do we make sense of these competing preferences when it comes to Radical Listening? To explore this question, we can turn to research on times when people naturally fall silent in conversation. Perhaps their silence is a signal that they are shielding themselves from the "slings and arrows of outrageous fortune" or maybe something else is going on. In one study, people attributed their spontaneous speechlessness to several principal reasons: they were surprised in the conversation, they felt anxiety or some other overwhelming emotion, or they lacked sufficient information to make a comment.[1] Those three reasons accounted for 75 percent of all explanations for falling silent in a conversation.

From this, we can infer that conversational silence serves a purpose. For example, if a person hears something surprising, silence buys them time to process the information and adjust. In instances in which a person does not know enough about the conversational topic to make a comment, silence gives them a chance to gather more information by listening attentively. In more extreme cases, keeping quiet might prevent a person from saying something stupid and risk looking foolish. In today's polarized world, silence can be a defense mechanism to protect ourselves from ridicule or attack. In short, silence in conversation is not nothing; it is something. And it clearly serves a purpose (or several).

One thing we can be certain of is that quiet is a precondition for good listening. Time and again, studies reveal that noise can serve as a distraction and lead to listeners missing critical information or having trouble understanding what they did hear. In the context of Radical Listening, it is tempting to think that this means that, to be better listeners, we should collectively try to control noise pollution. Although a quiet environment can support good listening, there is much more to it than that. In Radical Listening, quiet is both a verb and a noun. It is not only a state you are attempting to engineer; it is a specific skill you are employing as you listen.

In this chapter, we argue that the skill of quiet is something that you turn up and down in different settings and even within a single conversation. In the pages that follow, we will venture into the fascinating world of quiet. We will explore the topic of silence, tour the "quiet brain," and discuss some cultural dimensions of silence.

SILENCE

Let us begin with silence. In its most common usage, the word silence refers to a total absence of sound. This puts it on the extreme end of quiet, which simply refers to the absence of loud noises. For example, people are likely to be speaking in low voices to one another in a quiet zone on a train—although it is not silent, it is intended to be a low noise environment. In Radical Listening, we treat silence and quiet as relatively (but perhaps not completely) interchangeable. Common sense tells us that engaging in silence—or being quiet—allows us to concentrate on hearing through our ears and therefore listen well.

A cursory consideration of silence tells us that it is an important aspect of everyday conversation. Take the example of a pause—a momentary silence when a person is not speaking. Pauses come in the middle of speech, often signaling that the speaker is thinking about what they want to say. Pauses also come at the end of phrases and sentences. They can also signal that someone has finished speaking, inviting the listener to take their turn to share their thoughts. These examples of pauses—along with others such as "pregnant pauses," "to give pause," and "press pause"—suggest that silence is not a singular entity but something that comes in different shapes and sizes. There is attentive silence and companionable silence and the silence that comes with confusion.

In order to use silence as a skill it is, perhaps, helpful to consider types of silence and their many uses. If you Google "types of silence" you will find lists of varying lengths. Some writers suggest that there are seven types of silence whereas others favor nine types and one ambitious contributor even lists twelve. Let us be honest; these are just lists created by people to help us understand and think through the topic. They are not laws of nature, and we should not be enticed into believing that a list of any specific number is "the truth." Instead, we can learn to discern the differences from learning about typologies of silence that occur in conversations. To this end, the work of Dennis Kurzon is instructive.[2]

Kurzon, a professor of English language and literature, argues that in the context of conversation, there are several distinct types of silence. His list includes:

1. *Conversational silence.* This is what we usually think about in relation to being quiet in a conversation. It includes all the instances and reasons that a person might not speak. Here, Kurzon subdivides conversational silence into two smaller categories. The first is intentional silence, and it includes times when people choose not to speak. For example, if a person is confused or if they do not have sufficient knowledge about the topic of conversation, they might voluntarily

withhold commentary. Unintentional silence, by contrast, includes the natural hesitations and pauses that are part of conversation. Examples include thinking before you answer a difficult question or being quiet while you are trying to remember a person's name.

2. *Thematic silence.* Here, Kurzon suggests that people occasionally withhold commentary on a conversational topic they wish to avoid. When people choose silence rather than disagreeing, when politicians answer a different question than the one they were asked, or when a person quickly changes the subject, these are all examples of thematic silence. It is interesting to consider that in this type of silence a person might actually be talking. The silence refers to the topic being avoided rather than a lack of conversation.

3. *Situational silence.* Kurzon draws attention to the external factors that influence silence. Both conversational and thematic silences are related to psychological states and motives. Situational silence, on the other hand, refers to physical locations that encourage quiet. Places like bookstores, movie theaters, and museums. People are intuitively aware of how quiet they ought to be in various locations. You might whisper to a friend in the middle of a symphony performance, but you would not have a full-volume conversation such as you would at a party.

Where Radical Listening is concerned, we can simply flip Kurzon's types of silence and think about them as aspects of listening. For instance, great listeners will vary their own volume based on the context in which their conversation occurs. Further, they will pay attention to both what is said and what might be left out. Finally, they will track pauses within the conversation and interpret their meaning—is it time to be silent so that the speaker can think or is it time to jump in with a question or comment?

Building on the idea of *types* of silence, we can also explore *functions* of silence. Put in question form, what is silence for? The answer to this question is complicated because silence serves many functions in conversation and the purpose of silence is different for speakers than it is for listeners. Let us take each in turn, starting with the role of silence for speakers (see Table 4.1 for a list of the functions of silence).

It is a small irony that speakers are sometimes silent. Even when it is their turn to speak. If you pay attention to your everyday conversations, you will notice how much talk-free space—silence—there is within the interaction. Perhaps the most common type of speaker silence is when the speaker is thinking. This can happen right before they speak, as they gather their thoughts and consider how they want to make their point. It often happens in the middle of their speaking—even in the middle of a sentence—as they mentally search for a word. Finally, it happens at the end of their speaking, often to let their conversational partners know that they have finished speaking and the metaphorical podium is open for others. This last example is sometimes known as "procedural silence" because its function is to help the flow of conversation (in this case, to offer a signpost that it is time for a new speaker).

TABLE 4.1 The functions of silence in conversation

Speaker silences		Listener silences	
Type of silence	*Function of silence*	*Type of silence*	*Function of silence*
Selecting words	Communicative (helping to organize thoughts in order to make an effective point)	Speechless (from surprise or confusion)	To express an appropriate reaction; to buy time to form a more coherent response
End-of-turn pause	Procedural (helping advance the conversation)	Assent	To indicate agreement
Dramatic pause	To direct attention or cause tension	Avoidant (of controversy)	To maintain harmony with the speaker
		Listening	To support noticing and comprehension
		Emotional	To manage strong emotions

It may be that there is an almost primal function to a speaker's pause. Namely, that a moment of silence tends to invite listeners to lean in. We see this, especially, in a third category of speaker silence: the dramatic pause. This is when a speaker chooses to stop for a moment in order to build anticipation. It happens in stand-up comedy, in the beat before the punch line is delivered. It occurs when a speaker invites a listener to make a guess ("You know what happened then?") and it happens when we pause between words in a sentence to emphasize them ("I. Cannot. Believe. It!"). In this instance, speakers are using pauses for emphasis, directing their listeners to pay special attention. Sometimes the dramatic pause can happen even before the speaker starts to talk. Let us say someone has been asked a question. Figuratively, it is their turn to speak. But they do not say anything. This also builds tension. You may have noticed this during an argument with someone close to you. "What's wrong?", you might ask, passing the role of speaking to your conversational partner. They have heard the question, but there is no response. Drama ensues.

Silence is very different for listeners than it is for speakers. On the listening side of the conversational equation, silence happens in a wider range of instances and serves a greater range of purposes. For example, silence can be something that spontaneously happens to a listener, such as when they are astonished or confused. Please note that this is also good listening. When a listener is at a loss for words this can validate what the speaker has just said.

Similarly, silence can be something the listener chooses, such as when they want to pay careful attention to the speaker's words. Listener silence can also be communicative, as in the case that silence signals agreement or assent. Finally, silence can also be a strategy for avoiding controversy or disagreement with a speaker. The best listeners have an intuitive grasp of these various aspects of silence and they use them intentionally in their conversations.

CULTURE AND SILENCE

Anyone who has had the good fortune to travel will surely have noticed that societies around the world harbor very distinct norms related to the volume of sound. Visit a major city in India such as Kolkata or Mumbai and you will be treated to loudspeakers, honking, shouting, engines, and other high-decibel sounds. By contrast, visit Zürich and you will experience what the World Health Organization (WHO) identifies as the least noisy city in the world.[3] Even Tokyo, a metropolis of fourteen million people, is known for its relative quiet. It would not be surprising, then, to find that people from different cultures have their own norms for conversational silence. To the extent that this is true, it will impact the role of silence in Radical Listening.

When people from different cultures interact, they sometimes fall into communication problems. For example, Dutch people can seem direct—to the point of rudeness—to some Americans.[4] Americans, in turn, can come across as inauthentic in their positivity to some Dutch people. Cultures differ in the ways that they handle giving feedback, disagreeing, and many other aspects of conversation. One of these is the ways that cultural norms relate to silence.

Think about a time when you listened to a long period of silence. Maybe it was a long silence during a dinner or when a speaker paused for a long time during a work presentation. How did you feel? Some people are comfortable with silence and others find it awkward. In linguistics there are at least two theories that can help us understand these various reactions:

1. *Rules theory.* Each culture has a set of rules for how a conversation should unfold. This includes prescriptions for what is and is not appropriate to say, when it should be said, to whom things can be said, and how it should be said. Where silence is concerned, unwritten cultural rules determine how long it can last.

2. *Attribution theory.* This is a psychological theory that suggests that people make mental determinations about what is going on. This is especially true when we make guesses about the personality, motives, or experiences of other people. For example, when a person cuts you off in traffic, you might attribute their actions to their personality (they are a selfish, thoughtless jerk). Where silence is concerned, cultural norms influence the way that we make attributions toward silence such as believing that a person is ignorant, uncertain, weak, or passive.

You can see both of these theories in action by looking at the ways that Americans (on average) and Japanese people (on average) relate to and understand silence in conversations.[5] People from these two groups have divergent relationships with silence (see Table 4.2). In Japan, silence is viewed as a positive and active part of communication. Speakers and listeners may choose silence rather than upset social harmony by voicing disagreement. Listeners may also be more patient, allowing the speaker to be silent while they think of what they want to say and how they want to say it. Silence, then, is comfortable and respectful. By contrast, Americans place a premium on the pragmatics of speech. People are assumed to be direct and honest in their communication. Silence, then, can be seen as a failure of communication; as if the speaker were uncertain, inauthentic, or lacking in confidence.

TABLE 4.2 Silence in the United States and Japan

	United States	Japan
View of silence	It is passive communication, seen as unfavorable	It is active communication, seen as beneficial
Role of silence	It represents a communication failure: uncertainty, inarticulateness, or a lack of direct communication	It can be a useful way to avoid confrontation, it slows the pace of a conversation
Experience of silence	It can feel uncomfortable	It can feel polite and respectful

Researchers have found that Japanese people generally use longer pauses to signal a shift in speakers or a shift in conversational topic. This means that people engaging in Japanese rules of dialogue must pay greater attention to their context. What is the broad consensus of the group? What is appropriate to say? What is the best way of recognizing and respecting seniority and experience? This is known, in Japan, as "reading the air" and it is a measure of social adeptness. Being a great listener, in Japan, requires a person to listen to what is not being said, to be comfortable with silence, and to use silence as a valuable conversational tool.

Appreciating the beauty of silence is deeply ingrained in Japanese culture. The term "ma" refers to the silence between moments. The silence is significant because it creates a poignant pause that highlights the harmony, aesthetics, or beauty of what surrounds it. *Ma* can be experienced in Japanese Noh theater, in traditional tea ceremonies, and in traditional Japanese architecture. In all these contexts, silence is central to the experience of the listener, allowing them to feel a greater sense of balance and tranquility.

By contrast, Americans are more likely to overtly and verbally signal the shift in speakers or topics. One example of this is passing the turn to speak by posing a question such as "What do you think of that?" or "Right?" Another method is offering a transition phrase, such as saying "But anyway . . ." or "Well . . ." which are intended to cue the listener that the speaker desires a shift. Being a great listener, in the American context, means allowing speakers to express themselves. That is why, from this perspective, taking turns is important. Because language is viewed as a more practical tool for self-expression than is silence, listeners in the American context are focused on what *is* being said rather than the pauses or absences.

While on the topic of silence and culture, it is worth noting that deaf culture is one that communicates in the near or total absence of sound. This reinforces a central point of Radical Listening: namely, that listening goes beyond simply hearing. Listening is more than perceiving sound waves as they float through the air. In fact, the listening-as-hearing idea is a form of audism; the pejorative view that hearing people are superior to deaf people in our ability to communicate. To be sure, there are deaf people who would object to the use of the word "listen" because it is so historically intertwined with the world of the hearing.

That said, we use the term "listen" as do many linguists. We understand it as a constructive and collaborative act of communication—one that involves multiple sensory pathways and processes. Listening, in this broader view, entails looking, and responding, and noticing, and understanding. It includes attending to your own emotional reactions, to the interplay of physicality between the speaker and listener, and tracking shifts in the speaker. Regardless of whether a person can hear, they can still listen precisely because hearing is only the smaller part of listening.

CREATING SILENT SPACES

If silence is the foundation of great listening, then it makes sense that great listeners are more likely to harness quiet to effectively use their communication superpower. We all have experience with noise as obstacles to listening: the interruption of someone on their cell phone in a movie theater, or the difficulty of tracking a conversation in a loud café, or trying to talk to a friend while at a sports event. At work, ringing phones, chatty colleagues, computer pop-ups, nearby conversations, and other noises interfere with our ability to pay attention, let alone listen carefully. The quieter the context, the better the listening and, in turn, the better the conversation.

Quiet, in this way, can be thought of as existing on multiple levels. First, there is inner quiet. This is the serene mental state that allows a person to be focused on the conversation. Next, there is conversational quiet. This is a quiet that wraps around the conversation as it happens and can include promises of confidentiality, the experience of trust, or signaling that the conversation is important. Finally, there is environmental quiet. This is the noise—or lack thereof—in the physical location where the conversation occurs. We will discuss each of these in depth:

Inner Quiet

Whereas noisy cafés, honking horns, and crying children are examples of potentially distracting environmental noise, our so-called "inner chatter" can divert our attention just as much. Among the mental noise that can serve as an obstacle to great listening are our own emotional experiences. Some emotions, such as joy, anger, and surprise, are what psychologists call "highly aroused." They are, in essence, so loud that they can be difficult to tamp down. When we experience these feelings, there can be a temptation to blurt something out or to focus on the emotion rather than the speaker. Even low-arousal emotions such as boredom, irritation, or reverence can interfere with listening.

Fortunately, psychologists know a fair amount about how to manage emotions and this is a skill that can be taught and learned. Most of the discussion of this topic centers around tamping down feelings that are distressing, uncomfortable, or distracting. They include techniques such turning attention elsewhere, meditating, and relaxing your muscles. One of the tried-and-true ways of dampening emotional noise is diverting your attention. Ironically, listening is an example of exactly this! By getting out of your head and paying attention to what someone else is saying and how they are saying it, you can experience less emotional interference.

One way to manage interference during Radical Listening conversations is to become aware of what elite sports coach Tim Gallwey describes as the "inner game."[6] This refers to inner dialogue that can get in the way of our success. In tennis, for example, the outer game would be the match that you would observe—two players hitting the ball to one another over a net. The inner game takes place in the minds of each player. According to Gallwey, the inner game is played against self-limiting beliefs, lapses in focus, and self-doubt. A player's inner game can have a significant impact on their performance (the outer game). In other words, you are more likely to win the outer game if you conquer your inner game first.

In the case of Radical Listening, the inner game takes place within the minds of the listener and the speaker. Taking into account the importance of giving your conversational partner your full attention, it makes sense to work on managing your inner game so that it supports you to be at your best. See this list for a few ways to start working on your inner game:

- Notice your own self-talk. What are you saying to yourself when engaging in Radical Listening conversations? Are your own thoughts helping you to be fully focused on your conversational partner? If so, that is ideal. If not, there are a few things you can do.
- When you experience any lapses in focus, self-doubt, or unhelpful self-talk when you are engaged in Radical Listening, make a note of them and commit to some reflection time after the conversation. Then direct your attention back to your conversational partner.
- Challenge self-limiting beliefs. If you notice that your own self-talk is sometimes getting in the way, you can challenge your own thinking or work with a coach or mentor to support you to change some of your internal dialogue. This is not easy, and may take time, but it is possible and there are likely to be broader benefits for you.

• Take good care of yourself. You are much more likely to show compassion to yourself and your conversational partner if you are experiencing positive well-being. If you make sure that you give yourself what you need you are more likely to experience inner quiet.

Conversational Quiet

Conversational quiet is the quiet that surrounds a specific conversation. It does not refer to background noise in the physical environment—such as a cacophonous call center—but to the rules that govern a specific conversation. It is the social contract, often implied rather than explicit, that envelops a conversation in quiet. Perhaps the most obvious example of this is professional conversations that are formally protected by confidentiality. When lawyers, doctors, or psychotherapists have discussions with their patients or clients, there is a silence that wraps around those interactions. The knowledge that the exchange of information will be kept private helps the speaker to be more forthcoming and raises the ante on good listening. This extends, of course, to conversations that are not legally protected but which still require some confidentiality. Examples of this include a colleague who admits to planning to leave the company or being tipped off early about who is going to get the promotion.

Confidentiality is not the only form of conversational silence. Another instance of this is the absence of hidden agendas. If a conversation is transparent and authentic, it is not cluttered by the noise of office politics, grandstanding, or similar interference. This is a vital point for Radical Listening because it helps focus the listening. When a listener knows that the conversation can be taken at face value, they can commit more of their attentional resources to what is being said and fewer cognitive resources to figuring out why it is being said.

Environmental Quiet

In the 1980s, Bose Corporation unveiled a new technology for combating a noisy work environment: noise-canceling headphones. Originally intended for aviation, these devices neutralized the loud background whooshing of airplane noise. Several similar technologies have emerged: white noise machines, sound soothers, blue noise generators, soundproof panels, and soundproof acoustic pods that act as "silent rooms." Taken together, these devices suggest that many people are interested in creating oases of environmental quiet in an increasingly noisy world.

Indeed, occupational noise is problematic. In the United States, more than twenty million workers—principally those in construction, heavy industry, and similar jobs—are exposed to hazardous levels of noise.[7] Even in offices, crowding and electronics lead to unwanted noise. One interesting example of this is the noise level of hospitals. Rest and recovery in hospital is so important that the WHO has published guidelines for acceptable levels of "night noise." Hospital staff can also suffer from the cacophony of loudspeaker announcements, irregular beeping of monitors, device alarms, telephone calls, hydraulic doors, and other occupational noise. One study of nurses linked hospital noise to burnout, poorer work performance, and lower well-being.

This means that Radical Listeners are faced with the dual task of directing their attention to the speaker while also filtering out competing noise. It stands to reason, then, that reducing the environmental noise will help listeners focus better. To some extent, this is common sense and all of us have ducked into a quiet meeting room, turned off our cell phones, or shushed noisy neighbors.

Good listeners attempt to minimize distractions and Radical Listeners attempt to work in relatively quiet environments, signaling to the speaker the importance of the conversation. For example, great listeners might make a show of turning off their phones so that the speaker understands that what they are saying is the most important thing in the room. Similarly, they might tell an assistant to hold their calls or simply tell the speaker that the conversation will not be interrupted. You can see the subtle but powerful way that this leads to the emergence of norms for listening. In psychotherapy sessions, for instance, there is a universal understanding that nothing will interfere with the conversation. By contrast, many conversations at work—even important ones—are frequently interrupted.

One final note on environmental quiet. Radical Listeners take silent sound baths before entering crucial conversations. In advance of a team meeting, a one-on-one, or even a watercooler chat, great listeners take a moment to transition into listening mode. They often do this by stepping outside, closing their eyes, or ducking into an empty room. In each case, it is the quiet that helps put the person into the mindset of a terrific communicator, to center themselves, and to "put their ears on." Perhaps, most importantly, they remind themselves that the focus is on the speaker.

SUMMARY

Many years ago, the linguist Deborah Tannen wrote an article cleverly called "Silence: Anything But."[8] As this title suggests, the quiet moments in conversation are not just linguistic negative space. They are pregnant with meaning, they can be intentional, and they are tools both for listening and for communicating. One way that Radical Listening may differ from traditional notions of active listening is in the use of quiet and silence. Radical Listeners do not think of silence as the absence of conversation but as a skill to be employed in the best conversations. Active listeners are more likely to *stay* quiet while Radical Listeners *manage* quiet to create ideal environments for communication.

There are three aspects to the skill of silence: creating the environment to help listening occur, attending to silence to get more out of what is being said, and using silence strategically as a tool of communication. Regarding the first, Radical Listeners ensure that, to the extent possible, conversations occur in a quiet space—broadly understood—so that the conversation takes primacy. Great listeners notice silences on several levels including the natural pauses in conversation as well as topics that are avoided. Finally, Radical Listeners understand that even while being silent—remaining in the listening role—they can communicate agreement, acquiescence, hesitation, doubt, and many other conversational stances without saying a word.

QUESTIONS

1. How comfortable are you with silence in conversation? What do you notice about your reaction when silences happen? How do you think this helps or hinders the interaction?
2. In this chapter, we presented quiet as having many aspects: natural conversational pauses such as when a person searches for a word, communicating agreement or disagreement, or when a person is astonished and does not know what to say. How does thinking about silence in this way improve your understanding of great listening?

CHAPTER FIVE

ACCEPTING

History is of full of examples of listening failures. Poor listening is influenced by various factors. Take, for instance, the 1977 airport disaster in Tenerife, in the Canary Islands. It was on a day thick with fog when two 747s collided on the runway, killing more than 580 people. It remains the deadliest accident in aviation history. It is tempting to think that the captain, or someone in the control tower, was simply a bad listener, but the story is more complicated than that.

At 1 p.m. that afternoon, members of a separatist movement had detonated a bomb at an airport on a nearby island and planes were diverted to Los Rodeos Airport in the north of Tenerife, where the tragedy occurred. The facilities at Los Rodeos were quickly overwhelmed by all the unscheduled flights forced to land there and it is easy to imagine that the air traffic controllers might have felt overwhelmed.

One of the two planes in the accident was a KLM flight, headed toward Amsterdam. The crew was in danger of hitting their on-duty time limit—the number of hours a crew is allowed to work before they are required to rest. With the deadline and the delays of the day in mind, the captain of the KLM flight was eager to take off. Unfortunately, a Pan Am flight was preparing to take off at the same time, on the same runway. The fog prevented them from seeing one another.

When the KLM captain radioed the control tower with "We're going" the controller responded with "Okay, stand by for takeoff. I'll call you." Unfortunately, the Pan Am flight was radioed at the same time and their signal might have interfered with the KLM captain hearing anything other than "okay." The two planes began accelerating for takeoff from opposite sides of the same runway and collided.

With the vantage of hindsight, we can see that there were multiple factors at play—the unusual amount of air traffic, the thick fog, the anxiety provoked by an airport bombing, being at an unfamiliar airport, feeling time pressure, and breakdown in communications. Many of these related to an overlooked aspect of listening: accepting. Acceptance is a crucial internal skill in Radical Listening. It is also one of the least understood.

WHAT IS ACCEPTANCE?

What does it mean to accept what another person says? Does it suggest that we agree with them? That we value them as human beings? That we tolerate their ideas? In psychological science, researchers have viewed the concept of acceptance in terms of many interrelated ideas, such as non-avoidance and non-judgment.[1] In simple terms, it is the psychological acknowledgment of the situation as it is without trying to immediately make changes. In this way, acceptance is a foundational skill of listening because it emphasizes mental openness. Radical Listeners take in what is communicated without being distracted by their own judgments, biases, or agendas.

You can see, in the Tenerife airport disaster, that acceptance might have played a crucial role in averting the tragedy. For example, had everyone accepted the unusual events of the day they might have shifted from a "fly as usual" mindset to a slower one that prioritized safety over schedules. Had the captain of the KLM flight accepted the possibility that his crew might run out of time and that the flight might have to be canceled, he might not have rushed. If everyone had accepted the fact that the radio communications were unclear, they might have been more cautious. It is a difficult mental shift to make: it requires a person to put their goals and agenda momentarily aside, to slow down, and to openly take in what is communicated to them.

So, what is it—exactly—that we accept when we talk about acceptance as an aspect of Radical Listening? Here are four considerations:

1. Point of View

When in conversation, we listen better to others when we try to understand their point of view. Whether they are making a complaint, telling a story, or pitching an idea, it can be helpful to understand how they see things, what they are trying to accomplish, and what they expect from you. Accepting a person's point of view is distinct from *agreeing* with their point of view. You do not need to agree with the speaker—you are under no obligation to share their values, approve of their processes or behaviors, or take their side. If you want to listen well, however, you do have an obligation to try to understand their point of view.

Professional mediators understand this distinction well. Although they have a clear professional objective—to help the parties arrive at an agreement—they also understand that each participant in the process likely has an opposing viewpoint. Mediation works best when all parties—the mediator included—make an effort to understand and accept the right of each party to hold differing viewpoints. At least one study confirms this: participants who were instructed to "put themselves in their counterpart's shoes" had lower rates of hostility and bias.[2]

2. The Situation

People differ in their ability to accept the circumstances in which they find themselves. Whether it is a poor evaluation of job performance, falling behind a competitor, making a mistake in a presentation, or running late for work, it can be tough to swallow the pill of a tough situation. Acceptance implies acknowledging the situation exists, even if it is an uncomfortable or unsatisfactory one. It is the opposite of denial, where a person does not accept what is happening because it too difficult to process. Accepting that a situation is unfolding is not the same as being docile. You can readily acknowledge adverse circumstances and hope they change or influence them to the extent that doing so is within your control.

This relates to listening because it prioritizes understanding over personal agenda. By accepting situations as they occur, great listeners are able to acknowledge the feelings they stir, comprehend the factors and people involved, and appreciate various points of view. This situational acceptance can lead not only to better interpersonal listening but make way for more strategic and effective reactions.

3. Personal Limitations

It is not too hard to admit we are not perfect. We all make mistakes, regret some choices, and have some weaknesses. What is a bit more difficult to admit is that in every social interaction, we have some limitations. There is information we do not know, we harbor biases, we succumb to thinking errors, we occasionally labor under logical fallacies, and—sometimes—we are just plain wrong. When we accept these limitations, it opens the door to better communication. This type of acceptance leads to a shift from a negative inner monologue—critiquing the speaker, prioritizing our agendas, and inflexibly believing that we are correct—in favor of a learning mindset. When we adopt this perspective, we are more likely to be curious about the message being delivered and will ask questions if we do not understand something.

4. Pragmatism

Accepting the need to put things behind us can be transformative moments in our lives. It is easy to get caught in a trap of obstinacy and stubborn denial of this perspective. When we are hurt, feel that we have been wronged or insulted, it is understandable that we become defensive. This attitude usually leads to entrenched positions and can get in the way of reconciliation, collaboration, or progress. Radical Listeners can be accepting by adopting a pragmatic position. The key question is whether the relationship and the possibilities that may emerge from dialogue outweigh the desire to hold a grudge or redress a historical injustice. To put it another way, if we cannot set these desires aside, we make it impossible for us to engage in Radical Listening.

OBSTACLES TO ACCEPTANCE

In modern times, there are surprisingly few books on the art of acceptance. There are many on happiness, good leadership, and creativity, but far less on acceptance as a psychological process. Of those that exist, the vast majority are focused on mindfulness and meditation. Mindfulness practices are becoming increasingly popular—in part—because they are being presented in a secular way (their origins are in the Hindu and Buddhist traditions), and because they are widely effective, as a growing body of research shows. Engaging in daily meditation is not, of course, the only route to acceptance. Nor do such mindfulness practices offer a discussion of the common obstacles to acceptance. Here are three such obstacles, and you will likely be familiar with them from both your work and private lives:

Believing You Are Right

Perhaps nothing interferes with accepting another point of view as much as believing that your current point of view is correct. Every one of us harbors opinions based on our personal experiences and values. Our so-called "lived experience" can be so powerful that it can feel as if it is the sole reality. It is possible to recognize the validity of emotions and experiences even while understanding that others might have equally valid but contradictory experiences. Phrases such as "your truth" or "my truth" tend to conflate the concept of your experiences/opinions with some more profound universal truth. Once we have arrived at closure on our own position, it can serve as a deterrent to listening carefully and openly to others. What benefit could come from foreclosing on the rightness of our own experience? Either our interlocuter will agree with our position and reinforce what we believe to be true or they will disagree with it and we can thereby categorize them as being in the "wrong" camp.

Listening with the Intent to Rebut or Dismantle

Over time, each of us has developed a subset of communication skills that are central to arguing. For some of us, it is defensiveness, and, for others, it is going on the offensive. Regardless, it is common for people to listen with the intent to dismantle, rather than accept, the other person's statements. When this happens, we have a running commentary in our heads, sometimes silently practicing our rebuttals even while our conversational partner talks. When we are accumulating counterevidence, looking for argumentative weaknesses, and mentally rehearsing our own phrasing, we are not listening well nor are we accepting what is being said.

Politeness

It might sound odd to point out the potential downsides of politeness. After all, social niceties exist to help us interact and connect more smoothly. On the other hand, conversational etiquette can act like a distracting third party in a conversation. One of the most obvious examples of this is the common rule around turn taking in a conversation. First, it is your turn to speak, and when you are done it is my turn. What this occasionally leads to, however, is people checking out of a conversation and—instead of trying to understand—biding their time until it is their turn to talk. The unspoken mantra here is, "I don't need to listen; I simply need to wait until it is my turn." In the context of Radical Listening conversations, being overly polite might lead people to avoid challenging views or perspectives, even when they require further discussion. Politeness can lead to passive aggressive interactions in which the listener outwardly agrees with the speaker while being strongly opposed to what is being said.

In these obstacles, you can see a link between accepting what someone has to say and other critical listening skills. For example, if you do not engage in mental silence, you cannot hear enough, notice enough, or appreciate enough of what is being said to engage in acceptance.

HOW DOES ACCEPTANCE-ORIENTED THINKING WORK?

You cannot achieve acceptance—in the Radical Listening sense of the word—simply by removing obstacles. Instead, you must actively work on accepting. This means developing a foundational understanding of the mental processes related to accepting as an aspect of listening. You probably know some people who seem more naturally accepting than others. They have a certain openness about them. They are more likely to be flexible in their thinking, be open to opposing or diverging views, and be tolerant of ambiguity and uncertainty (see Table 5.1).

The three mental processes listed here are a nod to the idea that our heads are full of thoughts and cognitive processes every second of

TABLE 5.1 Being open and accepting

Quality	Definition	Example
Flexible thinking	Remains open to new evidence and can change one's stance	A leader decides to modify a sales strategy when new data suggest the current one is not working as well as hoped
Open to diverse views	Engages in intellectual exploration, works through confusion, and maintains curiosity about new views	A manager on an advertising campaign includes a team member who disagrees with the basic approach because the manager recognizes the potential value in the dissenting opinion
Tolerance of uncertainty	Is relatively comfortable in ambiguous situations and feels less pressure than others to arrive at final, singular conclusions	When faced with three possible product launch dates, a manager seeks feedback on which might be the best. When the first choice proves impossible, they calmly pivot to an alternative date, believing it will also work well

the day. We remember, perceive, plan, judge, estimate, solve, decide, envision, organize, learn, create, fantasize, recognize, and reason, to name just a few! Fortunately, these processes are automatic and natural to us—we do not need to think about doing them; we simply do them.

Two of these mental processes are directly related to our ability to accept. They are judgment and bias. Both words have a bad reputation. When people describe someone as judgy, for example, it is not a compliment. It means that they are opinionated, intransigent, superior, or disapproving. Not exactly what you want to list on a dating app to describe yourself! Similarly, people take a generally dim view of bias. People who are seen as biased are perceived to hold hidden agendas, to be dogmatic, or to be unfair. Interestingly, cognitive scientists—those who study these processes—take a more neutral view of them.

Judgment, from an academic point of view, is simply the mental act of evaluating something. When you say that you are proud of your child, that you enjoyed a meal, that you appreciate the contribution of your team members, or that you like one flavor of ice cream more than another, you are judging. It is as likely to be a positive evaluation as a negative one. Judgment, simply put, is the ability to discern quality or come to an opinion.

When you are engaged in Radical Listening, you are also engaged in judgment. It is unavoidable. Every time someone speaks, you evaluate their statements in terms of warmth, consistency, logic, clarity, motive, relevance, and credibility. You are judging, and it is beneficial to do so. It is what enables you to discern a good idea from a bad one, a liar from someone honest, and a confusing message from a clear one.

The downside of judgment, however, is that you can rush to closure on your untested opinions without first expending energy to be accepting. What might acceptance look like in this context? You would still be engaged in the same cognitive evaluation but you would make a conscious effort to take in the conversation from the other person's point of view. For instance, you might still judge whether their statements are warm or clear but you would also try to understand why they have arrived at those amounts of warmth or clarity. Are they a generally warm person? Are they angry? Do they understand the situation well? Have they thought this issue through in any depth? Each of those is an evaluative (i.e. judgy) question but one that is aimed at better understanding and accepting the other person.

We can take a similar approach to understanding bias. Psychologists define bias as systematic and predictable cognitive errors that influence judgments.[3] Let's take a simple example: imagine a neurosurgeon. Chances are, the person you pictured was male. If so, it does not mean that you are sexist or prejudiced. Instead, it is related to a series of common thinking shortcuts that are natural to all people.

Around the world, neurosurgeons are overwhelmingly male and so—in the absence of thinking of a specific neurosurgeon—people are more likely to envision one who conforms to "typicality" (meaning that your thinking is influenced by real-world base rates). There are dozens of these types of mental shortcuts and you can see ten common mental biases described in Table 5.2.

These types of mental shortcuts help us process information more quickly than we might otherwise.[4] Like judgment, they are neutral rather than "good" or "bad." Certainly, they can lead to mistakes, poor decisions, and can give rise to prejudice. On the other hand, they help us make mostly accurate decisions as quickly as possible.

Where Radical Listening is concerned, it can be helpful—vital even—to accept that you naturally engage in these mental processes.

TABLE 5.2 Ten common mental biases

Mental Bias	Definition
Confirmation bias	The tendency to collect evidence that supports your point of view while ignoring counterevidence
Hindsight bias	The tendency to believe events were predictable after they occurred
Overconfidence bias	The tendency to overestimate one's own abilities
Endowment effect	The tendency to overvalue something that belongs to you
Focusing illusion	The tendency to focus on a single detail and have it disproportionately influence your overall view
Counterfactual thinking	The tendency to compare real-world events to imaginary alternatives
Action bias	The tendency to prefer taking action over doing nothing
False-consensus bias	The tendency to believe that there is more agreement than there actually is
Negativity bias	The tendency to be sensitive to and likely to notice threats, problems, and setbacks
Fundamental attribution error	The tendency to underestimate the influence of situations on another person's behavior and to overestimate the role of personality

By being aware of them, you are better positioned to profit from their frequent benefits and to protect against their occasional drawbacks. Let us look at a specific example of each:

Profiting from Judgment

The entire process of hiring new employees is, essentially, one of judgment. Although it might be uncomfortable—especially for applicants sitting an interview—to think that they are being judged, that is exactly what happens. The candidate's résumé provides educational and past work experience that helps employers discern—or judge—whether they are knowledgeable and skilled. Moreover, prospective employers need to carefully evaluate candidates for personality fit, character, and other factors. Each of these criteria can represent a bias. For example, a team might prefer a humorous candidate over one who is seen as serious. In essence, they enter an interview listening for specific attributes such as evidence of a strong work ethic, the ability to take initiative, playfulness, or intelligence. By being aware of and transparent about these preferences, the group can profit from the best possible fit.

Protecting Against Bias

One of the lesser-known cognitive biases is called the "focusing illusion."[5] It is the tendency to emphasize—or focus on—one characteristic while overlooking other important factors. For example, if you were to guess the amount of happiness of a thirty-five-year-old lawyer who is currently going through a divorce, the divorce will likely have disproportionate weight in your mental calculus. You know that, generally speaking, divorce is an emotionally difficult time for people and so that detail might seem particularly relevant to the question of the person's happiness. It turns out that age is also correlated with happiness but your mental shortcuts likely (and accurately) process this as less important to happiness than divorce. Although this line of thinking is very often correct, it might be wrong. The person might be thrilled that they are leaving a painful relationship. To guard against possible blunders, you can simply ask for more information, such as inquiring "How are you feeling about it?"[6] Importantly, you will never consider doing this unless you recognize and accept that you have these biases in the first place.

THE CRUCIAL SKILLS OF ACCEPTING

It is easy for commentators to recommend that you acknowledge and accept the fact that you have a variety of biases. But the real question is, "How can people acknowledge and accept their own biases?" Fortunately, two well-researched areas provide exactly the tools we need to improve our acceptance quotients. Everything in this chapter up to this point has been context and knowledge. The usable takeaway skills begin here. They are "intellectual humility" and "curiosity." Both are key to being more accepting and, by extension, a Radical Listener.

Let us begin with intellectual humility. Like its conceptual cousin, regular old humility, it is an attitude of modesty. Intellectual humility is the understanding and acceptance that your thoughts and opinions might be wrong or otherwise limited.[7] A person who is high in intellectual humility can still hold strong opinions, offer reasoned arguments, and live according to their values. They recognize, however, that there might be holes in their knowledge or in their reasoning, and they acknowledge that other people might hold differing values.

Intellectual humility does not always come naturally, especially for people raised in Western cultures. Many of us are incentivized to present ourselves as knowledgeable (as opposed to clueless), consistent (as opposed to wishy-washy), and confident (as opposed to uncertain). Indeed, our peers reward us for our loyalty, our in-groups reinforce our like-mindedness, our colleagues expect us to be consistent in our views, and our work prizes our knowledge and decisiveness. Just consider who you would rather hire; the candidate who presents as a can-do person or the applicant who reveals that they are not really certain of anything and that there probably is not even such a thing as fundamental truth? Indeed, some experts argue that the opposite of intellectual humility—intellectual overconfidence—could be our default mental mode.[8]

Although there are social benefits to this mental bravado, there are numerous downsides as well. For example, people are susceptible to confirmation bias. Confirmation bias occurs when a person arrives at a conclusion and then pays attention only to evidence that reinforces that conclusion while largely overlooking any contradictory evidence. For example, a manager might foreclose on the idea that a particular employee is "difficult" and then be more likely to notice each instance of disagreement, tardiness, or substandard performance while failing to take equal stock of all the helpful and successful behaviors.

Another drawback is the natural risk of overconfidence. Take, for instance, knowledge of how a helicopter flies. If you had to rate your understanding of this topic on a 1–10 scale, where might you place yourself? Research reveals that people are surprisingly overconfident about this topic (and many, many others). What, for example, do you believe creates lift in a helicopter? Is it the downward push of air from the spinning rotors or might it be the way the rotors are shaped? It turns out that it is the latter and that helicopters are sucked up into the air through lift rather than pushing air down. Having understood that, what do you think makes the helicopter fly forward? There are, after all, no engines like you might see on a jet! What provides forward thrust for a helicopter? It is usually about this point that people start downgrading their original 1–10 rating! Our need to appear competent is not a phenomenon reserved to impress others; we often delude ourselves when it comes to the depth, breadth, and accuracy of our knowledge.

Intellectual humility works against these natural mental fallacies. It does so by focusing on two basic components of thinking:

- First, intellectually humble people recognize the limits of their knowledge. They understand that even experts do not know everything there is to know about a topic. They intuitively grasp that knowledge is dynamic and that there are always new facts, theories, and concepts emerging within any field of study. Ultimately, this leads to an openness to know more.

- Second, intellectually humble people recognize the fallibility of their ideas. They understand that all people are prone to biases, have prejudices, prefer their values, and are limited in their perspectives and experiences. The intellectually humble acknowledge that, at best, they provide opinions, incomplete arguments, and best guesses. Ultimately, this leads to an openness to take in new information and to hear opposing points of view and critiques.

Intellectual humility is more than showcasing modesty. Truly recognizing the limits of one's thinking is associated with a huge range of desirable benefits. The research on this topic has linked it with more civil discourse, reduced dogmatism, more open-mindedness, increased ability to forgive, greater levels of empathic concern, better ability to see a situation from another person's point of view, and greater ability to compromise.

The solution, then, lies in working against our tendencies to self-aggrandize by cultivating a sense of intellectual humility. Researchers have explored several techniques that have been shown to boost this quality. Admittedly, it is a small and emerging body of studies but it is promising nonetheless. There are three distinct approaches, each of which has received research support for boosting—at least temporarily—intellectual humility:

- *Self-distancing.* Several studies have revealed that when people evaluate their position from an alternative point of view, it helps their intellectual humility.[9] Coaches will be familiar with this meta-view technique as it often arises in questions such as, "If X person could hear the way you are describing this, what might she say?" Any technique that gets a person to look at an issue from another person's perspective can be a powerful tool for shedding light on biases and inconsistencies.

- *Humbling.* As the name suggests, any activity that humbles a person—where their own expertise and opinions are concerned—can boost intellectual humility. In one study, researchers had people write out their rationale for agreeing or disagreeing with a statement about a complex and technical issue: the potential economic benefits for Americans that might stem from trade between the United States and China.[10] It is easy to have a knee-jerk reaction based on political beliefs, personal experience, or cursory knowledge of the news. It is quite another thing, however, to have a sophisticated view based on knowledge of trade deficits, cost of labor, taxation and subsidies, and other economic issues. Having to contend with increasingly expert issues can shed light on one's middling knowledge and make people increasingly open to expert opinion. A second course of research explored the classic "consider the alternative" paradigm. Here, researchers asked participants to "consider the unknowns" (instead of "consider the alternative") and found that, across three studies, doing so lowered rates of overconfidence.

- *Growth mindset.* Finally, the understanding that both skills and knowledge are continually developing is linked to intellectual humility.[11] Although this might sound obvious, it is surprising how naturally we fall into the intuitive trap of thinking of our qualities as fixed traits. Intelligent people can view themselves as smart all the time, for instance. The same holds true for those who see themselves as socially intelligent, good managers, or creative. It is in our self-esteem interests to believe these qualities are reliable—you can count on them being there tomorrow, next week, and next year. However, all these qualities are variable. We have high-performance days and low ones, we continue to develop in new ways, even in areas of strength.

Regardless of whether intellectual humility comes naturally to you or you work at it, it is one of the most powerful tools of acceptance. Recognizing you own limitations—even for outstanding thinkers and experts—opens the door to listening to others and to accepting their experiences and values, even if you disagree with them.

The second crucial skill of acceptance is curiosity. Curious people generally seek out new information and experiences. One element of this thirst for the world is social curiosity. The socially curious are those people who love to drum up a conversation with strangers, who ask loads of questions, and who are careful observers of social behavior. People who are curious about others[12]

- report more pleasure from interactions;
- report more closeness after interacting with strangers;
- show lower levels of aggression toward others;
- appear to be less critical of others; and
- show less defensiveness when they are criticized.

This varies by culture and personality, to a degree, but it is also something that can be enhanced for those who want to invest in it. Over the last several decades, researchers have conducted a wide variety of interventions designed to create a spike in curiosity. One common method is by enhancing a sense of mystery. That is, by highlighting what is not known even as you are served up a helping of what is known. You have often been on the receiving end of such gambits:

movie previews tease out some information but leave some questions unanswered; clickbait headlines provoke a desire to find out more; novels end chapters with cliff-hangers; travel campaigns encourage you to discover unfamiliar places; a flirtatious smile might promise a great connection; gifts are hidden in wrapping paper; a scheduled event can generate buzz in advance of a product launch; and the list goes on.

You can use this technique on yourself when listening to another person by thinking of them as a mystery. As they speak, try focusing on the following types of questions:

- What do I not know about what they are discussing?
- What might they be leaving out?
- What else is there?
- Where is this conversation headed?
- What is this person's connection with the topic being discussed?

By treating your interlocuter and the discussion topic as if they are mysteries, you can easily boost your curiosity. If you choose to do so, you will be less likely to foreclose on your own impressions and opinions and more able to be open and accepting.

SUMMARY

There are so many common obstacles to accepting what another person has to say that it is a wonder that any listening happens at all. Despite these hurdles, there are two ways of thinking that can be crucial to acceptance. The first is intellectual humility: the idea that one's own way of thinking is not the only legitimate way of seeing things. The second is the lens of curiosity: being open to exploring new ideas before mentally foreclosing on a conclusion. Importantly, accepting what someone else says is not the same as agreeing with it. Through acceptance, you are demonstrating a willingness to hear them out and to consider their thoughts, even if you do not approve of or support their conclusions.

QUESTIONS

1. Each of us has topics about which we are more or less likely to accept divergent viewpoints. What have you noticed about the instances in which you are the most accepting of other perspectives? What about the instances in which you are least likely to be accepting?

2. What do you notice about your own curiosity? When are you highly curious and when do you cast curiosity aside? What do you notice about the ways that curiosity affects your interactions?

3. How might awareness of your own thinking biases improve your ability to listen?

· · • • ● ● ● ● ● ● ● • · ·

PART THREE

EXTERNAL LISTENING SKILLS

In this section, we shift our focus to the three behavioral skills of listening. We begin with a discussion of acknowledging. Acknowledgments are small nods, sounds, and statements intended to validate another person, celebrate them, or demonstrate engagement. Here, we explore seven distinct levels of acknowledgment and make recommendations for how (or how not) to use each. Next, we tackle the mainstay of active listening: asking questions. It might sound ironic that questioning is core to listening because when you are asking questions you are talking rather than listening. When used effectively, however, questions are short and relevant, and invite more talking from the other person (and, therefore, more listening on your part). Questions are also a surefire way to demonstrate that you are interested and paying attention. We discuss types of questions and common obstacles to asking great questions. We conclude this section with a discussion of interjecting. The idea that interrupting is a part of great listening is, perhaps, the most counterintuitive aspect of Radical Listening. Indeed, talking over another person can be extraordinarily rude. Here, we recast interjections as fast, strategic, and often helpful to conversations. It includes asking follow-up questions, making jokes, inserting observations, and guessing. In each instance, the listener immediately returns the podium to the speaker. In some ways, it is the most artful aspect of being a Radical Listener.

CHAPTER SIX

ACKNOWLEDGING

At its core, Radical Listening has the intention of deeply acknowledging other human beings. That is what gives Radical Listening its power. The conversation is a vehicle for showing respect and demonstrating positive regard for others. We acknowledge others by offering them the recognition and respect they deserve. When you engage in Radical Listening, you are providing your conversational partner with evidence that they matter.

In this chapter, we make the case for acknowledgment as a key aspect of Radical Listening. We begin with an exploration of research and theories that offer us a foundational understanding of why acknowledging people can be so effective in building and maintaining relationships. We know that human beings are "wired" to connect with one another—through verbal and nonverbal cues and explicit and implicit interventions. To delve into how human beings connect with one another, we first consider the seminal work of the best-known thought leader in the art of successful marriages, John Gottman. Then we consider the work of Shelly Gable who has been researching the impact of "active constructive responding" (ACR) for over a decade. ACR is a reliably positive way of responding to others when they have good news to share. Then, we view conversational interactions from a positive psychology lens to see how character strengths and the use of appreciative inquiry add to our understanding of how we can bring out the best in our conversational partners. Finally, we present our own framework. The Seven Levels of Acknowledgment framework will provide you with practical, implementable ways of bringing appropriate acknowledgment into your conversations. We conclude the chapter with immediately adoptable terms and phrases that can be built into your conversational repertoire.

KEEPING IT REAL

Before starting, let us reflect briefly on the role that acknowledgment has played in your life. Specifically, recall a moment in your life in which you felt energized because you knew that you were truly valued. Once you call a moment to mind, recall it in as much detail as possible:

- Who was it that acknowledged you?
- How, exactly, did they do so?
- What impact did the acknowledgment have on how you view this person?
- Who did you share the acknowledgment with, if anyone?
- How do you feel right now as you remember this?

It is likely that the moment you remembered was the result of a person, a group of people, or an organization acknowledging you or your contribution. It is also probable that you felt good at the time you were acknowledged and good in the present moment as you recall this time. The purpose of developing the skill of acknowledging is to give other people exactly these types of experiences and feelings.

BREAKING UP MAY BE HARD TO DO, BUT IT IS EASY TO PREDICT

Imagine showing up at a psychology research lab along with your romantic partner. After checking in, you are asked to discuss an area of ongoing disagreement in your relationship while the scientists videotape your interaction. This is exactly what John Gottman and his colleagues did with hundreds of couples across many studies and years.[1] They were principally concerned with the quality of the marriage (the couples in his original studies were always heterosexual and married).

Gottman looked at the ways wives and husbands interacted. The researchers paid attention to body language, touching, expression of emotion, and other aspects of communication. After systematically evaluating the various interaction styles, and following up over time to see who remained married, Gottman made a bold claim: he could accurately predict which couples would stay together and which would get divorced simply by watching these short interactions.

People disagree in many different ways. Some shout, others fume. Some plead, others lay out systematic arguments. The researchers found that a few of these styles were particularly toxic to relationships. Namely, holding the other person in contempt or being overtly critical of them were both deemed to be damaging in the long term. Similarly, emotionally withdrawing and being overly defensive reliably led to calamitous results. What is more, positive styles of interaction were important to the health of the relationships.

Gottman and his coauthor, Nan Silver, argued that people would reach out to one another (they called these interactions "bids").[2] Bids are interactions that are used to build strong connections. According to Gottman, these bids are attempts to build connection, gain the interest, or attract the attention of the other person. Based on observations in their laboratory, Gottman saw that bids could be accepted or rejected. Accepting bids tended to strengthen relationships while rejecting them damaged relationships. Gottman identified three responses: "turning away" (ignoring); "turning against" (responding with hostility); and "turning towards" (responding with enthusiasm).

Responding with enthusiasm aligns well with our skill of acknowledgment. Here, we do not necessarily mean high-fiving people and whooping like a fan at a sports match. Instead, we suggest that taking the time and truly communicating to another person that they have done well, celebrating their success, or otherwise giving them an overt nod, can be positive for them and for the relationship.

This can be seen in another program of research, this time conducted by Shelly Gable and her colleagues.[3] These scientists were, like the Gottman team, interested in healthy relationships. Gable and her colleagues also invited couples into their laboratory but they focused on a slightly different question: instead of focusing on moments in which things go wrong, they wanted to explore how people react when things go right. Specifically, Gable and her team were interested in how people celebrated their partner's good news, such as a promotion at work.

To do so, they divided potential responses into one of four conceptual categories based on how enthusiastic and how positive they were (see Table 6.1). The enthusiasm dimension includes active responding (having a stronger response) and passive responding (having a muted

TABLE 6.1 Active constructive responding

	Active	Passive
Constructive	Overt celebration ("Wow, I knew you could do it")	Muted positive comment ("Oh, nice")
Destructive	Overt criticism ("I'm surprised. You don't seem at all qualified!")	Covert criticism ("A promotion? Are you sure you'll be able to handle that responsibility?")

response or no response). The positive dimension including constructive responding (saying celebratory things) and destructive responding (saying dismissive things).

As you might guess, the active constructive responses (ACR) were associated with the healthiest relationships. ACR requires people show authentic interest in what the other person says while listening actively. The listener is expected to provide good eye contact, nod regularly, display encouraging facial expressions, and open body language. They are also expected to provide a supportive response (or, acknowledgment). By focusing on the positives of what your conversational partner says, and showing enthusiasm for their ideas, you make them feel better about their successes. Gable recommends explicitly complimenting strengths and saying things that help to amplify achievements. Of course, it is important to do so in ways that are culturally authentic.

An example of cultural variation in positive listening can be seen in the example of strengths. All people have strengths. Some people are organized, others creative, charismatic, or loyal. Although each of us has a set of natural strengths, not everyone is equally comfortable discussing them openly. People from some cultures, such as those that promote humility, might be ill-at-ease when they are singled out for their strengths or successes. By contrast, people from highly individualistic societies might relish being acknowledged for their uniqueness.

Regardless of cultural leaning, all people thrive on some form of acknowledgment. There are cultural differences about how and when people like to be acknowledged. It is also helpful to remember that strengths are not only an opportunity to shine—they can also be used to contribute. For people in high-humility societies, active constructive responding might be more effective if the celebration is couched in terms of their contribution to a group or an organization.

THE SEVEN LEVELS OF ACKNOWLEDGMENT

Based on the research of communication and relationship experts, what we are learning from the field of positive psychology, and our own experience as executive coaches and educators, we have developed a nuanced framework that sets out the levels of acknowledgment that can be experienced in conversations (see Figure 6.1). The purpose of this framework is to elucidate the range of interventions available to you when you are engaged in Radical Listening. Presenting the interventions in this way helps to operationalize the use of acknowledgments in conversations and allows you to develop your skills and tendency to use the appropriate level of acknowledgment when listening to others. The framework categorizes the interventions from the most damaging to relationships (at the bottom) to the most constructive (at the top).

We will set out each of the levels of acknowledgment with a clear explanation of each, followed by an example and then commentary about their use in conversations and a recommendation of their use when engaging in Radical Listening conversations.

Denouncing: Rejecting or Disputing Experiences or Emotions

We use the term *denouncing* to refer to an intervention that involves rejecting a person's perspective, view, experience, or emotions. In the context of Gottman's theory of bids, denouncing is an aggressive form of "turning against" because it is confrontational. One person is disputing the validity or accuracy of the other person's responses. Gable would categorize this as an "active destructive response"—the opposite of the kind of response most conducive for Radical Listening. When denouncing occurs, it can turn a conversation into a confrontation, rather than a dialogue. Emotions will run high and both parties are likely to harden their positions and become defensive.

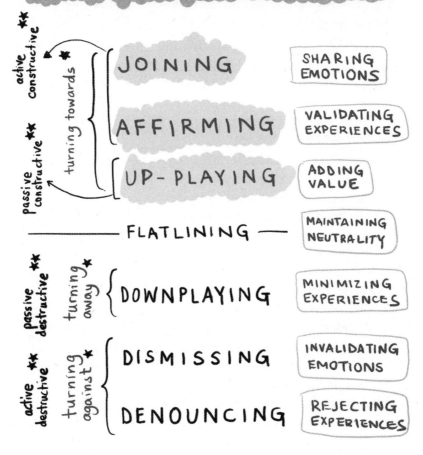

FIGURE 6.1 The seven levels of acknowledgment
Source: Original artwork by Christian van Nieuwerburgh

Usually driven by strong personal views, denouncing is the most extreme form of *not* acknowledging the other person's views or perspective. On the receiving end, it can feel like the person disagrees with your view *and* that they do not care about you or your feelings. When should this be used in Radical Listening? Never. There is no place for denouncing in Radical Listening, where the intention is always to show people that they are valued and that their opinions are welcome.

EXAMPLE OF DENOUNCING

Manager 1: "What should we do about morale in the organization?"

Manager 2: "That's a good question. It's obvious we need to address it in some way. I feel a bit guilty for letting it fester. Hoping that it would resolve itself was naïve. I would like to call everyone together, admit that we've taken our eye off the ball and invite them to work with us to improve well-being across our business."

Manager 1 [denouncing]: "Seriously? Sometimes, I can't believe that you've made it to a leadership position. It's obvious that if we did that, it would make things so much worse. We're not responsible for everyone's happiness! Everyone needs to take responsibility for how they feel. Let's not make it worse by pandering to their incessant complaints."

Manager 2 [defensive response]: "Sometimes, I think it's your hard-nosed approach that gets in the way of us doing anything to make it better. It's not pandering to be interested in the well-being of our people!"

Dismissing: Actively Invalidating Experience

We use the term *dismissing* to refer to invalidating another person's ideas, concerns, perspective, or emotions. Although is not as antagonistic as denouncing, it is still a form of *not* acknowledging. When you dismiss another person's views or emotions, you are not accepting them as valid. Dismissing refers to not accepting what the other person is saying without presenting an alternative view or perspective. Using Gottman's theory, this is another, less confrontational way of "turning against." Based on Gable's work, dismissing could be understood as destructive.

The most harmful aspect of dismissing is that the speaker does not feel heard or understood. It is likely they will want to withdraw from the conversation. Dismissing is likely to damage rapport in the moment that it occurs. Longer term, it can even degrade the quality of the relationship between the two people. To be dismissed causes people to question their own competence or value, leading to doubt, resentment, or anger. There are four common ways this happens:

- Dismissing the gravity of the situation: The listener glosses over the gravity of the situation, suggesting that the speaker may be exaggerating.
- Dismissing the uniqueness of the situation: The listener does not appreciate how unique the situation feels for the speaker, suggesting in their response that the situation is common or that it happens to many people.
- Dismissing the focus on the other person: The listener takes attention away from the speaker by talking about their own situation or response.
- Dismissing the relevance of the topic: The listener questions how the topic of conversation is relevant to the discussion.

When should this be used in Radical Listening? Dismissing is to be avoided because Radical Listening is an intervention that is designed to appreciate people. We should accept the speaker's assessment of the gravity of the situation and their sense that the situation feels unique to them. In Radical Listening, the focus should always be kept on the speaker. At no point should your conversational partner feel that their topic is not important or relevant.

EXAMPLES OF DISMISSING

"Wow! Coming back to the office after working from home for so long has been harder than I thought! It's caught me by surprise. My quality of life has been really affected. I don't get as much time with my children as I would like, I have no flexibility during the day, and then I am spending almost an hour getting home in the traffic. I wonder if I should talk to the Human Resources team about this? I'm feeling really low, and I'm sure it will start affecting my work."

Different forms of dismissing:

Response 1 [dismissing the gravity]: "Don't be such a drama queen! You've only been back for a week. I'm sure you'll settle back into the routine. Give it a couple of months and you'll be back to your usual self."

Response 2 [dismissing the uniqueness]: "Talk to HR? Join the queue! We're all experiencing the same things. You know Dom, right? He asked for a day a week to work from home and they said no. It's best if we keep a low profile for a couple of months. Maybe if we raise this later in the year, management will be more flexible."

Response 3 [dismissing the focus]: "I know exactly what you're saying! I'm feeling the same. I never see my kids anymore! And I wish it took me an hour to get home. On a bad day, it's more like two hours for me. I've decided to hand in my notice. I'm better off finding another job closer to home."

Response 4 [dismissing the relevance]: "OK, I get that. But we only have thirty minutes together and we should really be talking about our work project. Did you get that email that I sent you?"

Downplaying: Minimizing the Significance of Experiences or Emotions

We use the term *downplaying* to refer to minimizing talk about particular topics. Using Gottman's theory, this would fall under the category of "turning away," whereas Gable would see this intervention as passively destructive. Downplaying is damaging because it minimizes the opportunities for your conversational partner to talk about things that are important to them. When you are downplaying, you are assessing ideas, emotions, and topics as being of less value that the speaker suggests.

When should this be used in Radical Listening? Almost never. Downplaying a person's strengths, concerns, or values can be damaging to the relationship. Downplaying can also be problematic because it becomes more difficult to prioritize and allocate value if things are minimized. There might, however, be rare exceptions in which downplaying a situation (rather than a person) can have strategic value.

EXAMPLES OF DOWNPLAYING

Colleague 1: "I'm genuinely glad that our team won the national award for diversity, equity and inclusion. But I was disappointed with the speech by our director. She focused mostly on her own contribution and singled out my colleague for praise without mentioning me at all. I spent more time than anyone on this and it was originally my idea to apply for this award. It seems like my work has not been recognized. Maybe I need to be more vocal about my contributions—but you know me, I don't like singing my own praises . . ."

Colleague 2: "Well, you can be proud to be part of the team that won a national award! And you know the contribution that you've made. Isn't that enough?"

EXAMPLES OF FLATLINING

Colleague 1: "Before we get too far into this project, we should consider the risks and worst-case scenarios. I mean, do we even know the background of our proposed partner organization? I've never heard of them. And then, we should do a full risk assessment—not only financially but also from a reputational perspective. I'm usually less cautious but I have an intuition that we need to move slowly on this."

Colleague 2: "Yes, of course, we should go into this with our eyes open. But we don't want to get left behind. Let's get started with the partnership and ensure that we review how things are going."

Flatlining: Adopting a Completely Neutral Attitude

The term *flatlining* refers to displaying no obvious reaction to what is said. Its purpose is to avoid influencing a person in any way. In other words, a person on the receiving end of flatlining would not be able to easily decipher the listener's opinion or judgment about what has been said. Flatlining is sometimes used

- to withhold a perspective that might be distracting or lead to conflict. For instance, a listener might remain neutral if the speaker off-handedly mentions a political issue with which the listener disagrees but which is also not central or important to the conversation.
- to avoid reinforcing an unwanted direction in the conversation. For example, of all the levels of acknowledgment, this is the one that is most neutral—the listener does not encourage or discourage their conversational partner. This level does not sit comfortably within the Gottman framework, as it is not, strictly speaking, turning away—and yet it is not turning toward either.

Flatlining is also difficult to categorize using Gable and Reis's terminology. It is definitely "passive," but flatlining is intentionally neither destructive nor constructive. It conveys a sense of objectivity and neutrality in the listener which is useful at certain points in Radical Listening conversations.

When should this be used in Radical Listening? Rarely. Flatlining should be used judiciously when engaging in Radical Listening. There is a risk that flatlining can be interpreted as a lack of interest or rejection of ideas. The use of flatlining should be reserved for situations when you are responding to strong emotions or controversial views that may not be pertinent to the conversation. Flatlining is a bid to stay in the conversation and preserve the relationship when dealing with sensitive topics.

EXAMPLES OF FLATLINING

Colleague 1: "I'm furious. I cannot believe they said that about me. Were you there when they called me uncooperative? That's just typical. I've had enough of this nonsense. I'm going to go over there right now and give them a piece of my mind. I won't hold back. They've crossed a line this time!"

Colleague 2: "I wasn't there, so I cannot really comment on what was said."

Colleague 1: "The situation is so bad right now. People deny it, but immigration is part of the problem. Uncontrolled immigration is flooding public services and local people are getting squeezed out. I'm starting to think that we need to be more vocal about preserving our culture and traditions."

Colleague 2: "It sounds like your concerns about immigration make you think that you need to speak up about preserving your culture and traditions."

Up-Playing: Adding Value Through Short Summaries or Signals

The term *up-playing* refers to minimal conversational inputs that demonstrate your engagement in what is being said. As the name suggests, the listener shines a conversational spotlight on the speaker's words. Perhaps the most common version of this is when a listener plays back some aspects of what they have heard, as in the comments "It sounds like this is really important to you" or "Yeah, that does seem unfair."

A slightly more powerful alternative builds on these basic acknowledgments by adding value and interpretation. Here, a listener might thematically summarize what is being said or connect it to something larger. For example, after a colleague worries about an upcoming event, you might distil their comments with an educated guess, such as responding, "It's clear you want things to go well because you are so heavily invested in this event and because you recognize that it will reflect on your entire team."

The purpose of up-playing is to acknowledge something your conversational partner has said without interrupting the flow of the conversation. Because it is less active than affirming or joining, this could be considered passive constructive responding (Gable) or the mildest form of "turning towards" (Gottman). Up-playing is a low-cost, nonintrusive way of building rapport and showing interest in what your conversational partner is saying. It can also be used to prioritize focus on more positive aspects of a topic or situation.

When should this be used in Radical Listening? Frequently. Up-playing is an effective technique that conveys interest and can direct attention without disrupting the conversation. This can be used often during Radical Listening because it is a subtle and nonintrusive way of acknowledging.

EXAMPLE OF UP-PLAYING (NOTING)

Colleague 1: "It's pretty busy at the moment, with multiple priorities colliding. I can't remember the last time I had a full night's sleep."

Colleague 2: [Furrows their eyebrows and purses their lips.]

EXAMPLE OF UP-PLAYING (PRIORITIZING)

Colleague 1: "I don't know whether to apply for the promotion this year or not. My manager advised me not to apply last year. She said that I needed more experience. It's a year later, and I've been making great progress. Sometimes, though, I don't know whether I'm up for a job with more responsibility. You know me—I love my freedom, and I can be disorganized and scatter-brained sometimes! Not really leadership qualities!!"

Colleague 2: "It sounds like you made good progress this year! What would you need in order to feel more confident about applying?"

Affirming: Explicitly Commenting on Your Recognition of the Topic

We use the term *affirming* to refer to the act of explicitly stating that you recognize something in what your conversational partner is saying. This is not a fleeting nod. It is an active intervention from the listener to set out very clearly that they value, recognize, or appreciate something about their conversational partner or their topic. Gable would consider this the standard active constructive response, and Gottman would recognize this as a concrete way of "turning towards." When people think about acknowledging other people, they are most often thinking about this level of acknowledgment:

affirming by saying something that conveys appreciation, interest, or compassion.

When should this be used in Radical Listening? Occasionally. This is the least ambiguous form of acknowledgment so it should be used consistently in Radical Listening. However, because it is so explicit, there is a risk that it can sound insincere if overused during conversations.

EXAMPLES OF AFFIRMING

Colleague 1: "Completing a university degree while working full time has been a greater challenge than I expected. Don't get me wrong, I still think it was the right decision and I'm loving the course. But finding the time to do everything—work, family, exercise, and study—that's been more of a challenge than I thought it would be."

Colleague 2: "I really admire you for always investing in your professional learning. You'll have to give me some tips on how to do it!"

Colleague 1: "I got that job that I was talking to you about!"

Colleague 2: "I'm not surprised. You worked really hard on the application."

Joining: Getting Involved in the Experience or Emotion

We use the term *joining* to refer to the highest level of acknowledgment. This goes beyond commenting or appreciating. When you join your conversational partner, you are partaking in the experience or emotion. You become part of the celebration, commiseration, or emotional response. This can range from crying alongside your conversational partner to dancing around with joy and excitement. This is the most effusive form of "turning towards" (Gottman) or the most active way of responding constructively (Gable). From your conversational partner's perspective, it will feel like you fully support them and that you share in their experiences and emotions.

When should this be used in Radical Listening? Occasionally. This is a very high-energy style of interaction. At its best, it can strengthen rapport because you feel what your conversational partner feels. There is little that is more validating to a speaker than letting them know you are touched by the same emotions they feel. However, there are certain risks associated with joining. First, overuse should be avoided because there is a risk that you can overshadow your conversational partner if you become more animated than they are. Second, there might be instances in which you need to remain emotionally distant from a situation so that you can offer a perspective less encumbered by strong feelings.

EXAMPLES OF JOINING

Colleague 1: "It's happening! We're going ahead with our leadership retreat to Hawaii!"

Colleague 2: "Woo-hoo [jumps up and offers a high five]! Hawaaaaiiiii!"

———

Colleague 1: "One of my mentors has passed away. I'm devastated that I never had the chance to tell them how much they impacted me [starts crying]."

Colleague 2: "They were amazing. I can't believe they're gone forever [wipes away a tear]."

THE LANGUAGE OF ACKNOWLEDGMENT

There are no hard and fast rules for how to acknowledge another person. Effective validation will vary depending on personality traits, cultural leanings, language spoken, and how casual or formal a relationship is. Even so, there are some general guidelines that might

TABLE 6.2   Phrases that help

I get what you mean	This is a very simple way of telling your conversational partner that you understand them, even if you do not have the same experience as them.
I hear you	This common phrase captures the very essence of acknowledgment. It is a clear and explicit statement that you are paying attention and considering what they have to say.
I notice that you . . .	By sharing what you notice with your conversational partner, you are demonstrating your engagement. You might not always be correct in what you notice but people generally appreciate the attentiveness.
It sounds like . . .	By playing back what you are hearing, you provide proof that you have been listening carefully. This is especially useful when paired with an observation about their values, experience, or point of view.
I love how you . . .	This is a clear and explicit way of showing your appreciation of your conversational partner and how they are managing their situation.

TABLE 6.3   Phrases that hinder

It seems to me that . . .	Although this appears to be attentive, this statement actually shifts away from your conversational partner's thoughts and feelings. Instead, you pivot to discuss your own reactions and interpretations.
If you want my opinion . . .	By proposing your own opinion, you are taking focus away from your conversational partner's perspective.
If I were you . . .	This hypothetical proposition is usually of little value. In this case it distracts attention from your conversational partner.
Don't overthink it	Even though the intention might be positive, this minimizes the challenge faced by your conversational partner and criticizes their response to it.
It will all be all right	It sounds like a statement designed to reassure your conversational partner but it can feel dismissive of their concerns as well as unrealistic.

help you practice and develop this skill. There are, in English, certain phrases that are more likely to build connection (see Table 6.2) whereas there are others that run the risk of damaging connection (see Table 6.3).

SUMMARY

Acknowledging is a foundational skill of Radical Listening. Not only does it show that you are interested in your conversational partner, it can boost their self-confidence and well-being too. Understanding the various levels of acknowledging will allow you to contribute positively to conversations, and be intentional about what will be most helpful with different conversational partners and at certain points in your interactions.

QUESTIONS

1. How comfortable are you being on the receiving end of acknowledgment? How do you like to be validated or celebrated?
2. What experiences have you had with active constructive responding? For example, can you think of times when you felt dismissed because your contributions were recognized but minimized? What opportunities do you see to use this approach to respond to the good news of others?
3. Which of the seven levels of acknowledgment is most interesting to you? Why?

QUESTIONING

Whether a person speaks Spanish or Swahili, Turkish or Tagalog, English or Esperanto, they ask questions, although each language does so in its own way. In Spanish, it is common to end a statement with a question—called a "tag"—such as when a person says "*¿Muy interesante, no?*" (Very interesting, right?). By contrast, Mandarin speakers occasionally contrast a positive against a negative by way of asking about a choice. For example, they might ask you what would—in English—translate as "Do you want/not want?" In English, we have standard words such as *who, which,* and *where* to indicate a question. There are also archaic question words that have fallen out of fashion since the time of, say, Shakespeare. For example, we do not spend a lot of time losing sleep over "*whither*" we might go or wringing our hands about issues such as "*Wherefore* art thou, Romeo?"

Linguists recognize questions as being central to our ability to communicate with one another. Termed "interrogatives" by academics, questions are a type of sentence or phrase that is designed to gather information or seek clarification. When we ask the time, consider which choice is superior, wonder about the cause of an event, ask for an opinion, or inquire whether our pet dog is a good boy, we express the curious, not-knowing sentiment that is at the core of all questions.

The ability to question has probably been part of the human experience since the emergence of language itself. As language developed, it became useful to distinguish between *when* something might be done and *how* something might be accomplished. From the evolutionary perspective, the groups who were able to ask one another questions such as "*Where* is the best fishing?" or "*What* is on the other side of that hill?" were better able to gather data, make good decisions, and adapt to their surroundings. Similarly, asking questions such as "What are your intentions?" or "What do you need from me?" also facilitated stronger social connections and better cooperation within early human communities. In every case, communities that developed questions were more likely to survive.

Although it may seem plausible that questioning is vital to communication, it may not be immediately obvious how questioning is an essential part of Radical Listening. Intuition might tell you that asking questions is the *opposite* of listening. In fact, when a person asks a question verbally, they seem to be talking rather than listening. However, posing a question is only a temporary moment within a broader back-and-forth of conversation. Taking the turn to speak, in the form of asking a question, sets up your conversational partner to do more speaking and places you in a position to do more listening. The aspect we would like to focus on is how each question posed by the listener is an invitation for the speaker to share more.

THE BASIC STRUCTURE OF QUESTIONS: THREE CATEGORIES

Most of us have learned that questions have two basic structures: open and closed. Closed questions, by this way of thinking, are those that call for a yes or no answer. For example, when we ask "Are you allergic to peanuts?" or "Do you have the slides ready for today's pitch?" we are not looking to engage in a rich conversational tête-à-tête. Instead, we are hoping to get a quick piece of information. Closed questions are about efficiency much more than they are about great listening. Closed questions tend to start with certain words such as "do," did," "could," "would," and "are." By contrast, open-ended questions are, supposedly, those that invite a much more in-depth response. These questions tend to start with "who," "what," "when," "where," "why," and "how."

Let us do away with this traditional view of two types of questions or, at the very least, modify it. The rationale for doing so can be seen in the fact that many so-called open-ended questions act exactly like the closed ones. For instance, if someone asks his supervisor "When is this report due?" it is a bid to clarify information. His boss might respond with "by the end of the day" or "at five o'clock" or "before you leave," but, in any case, the response options are limited. Here we can see that there is, at the very least, a third category of questions that we can think of as "narrowing questions." Narrowing questions inquire about a limited range of answers but are not as singular in their focus as closed questions. Questions beginning with "who," "where," and "when" are often narrowing questions (although they can be open-ended questions in some circumstances).

Questions starting with "why" and "how" are typically the most open in that speakers have the widest leeway in how to respond to them. This does not mean that great listeners must confine themselves to these two questions. Each type of question serves a certain purpose but those that offer latitude in responding are also those that offer the best opportunities for listening (see Table 7.1).

TABLE 7.1   Three categories of questions

Category	Benefit	Example
Closed questions		
A. Alternatives	Expedient way to get information while also offering choice	"Would you rather take the lead on this project or have me do it?"
B. Tags	Expedient method for checking a hunch or guess	"You want to take the lead, right?"
C. Content	Expedient way to get a clear answer	"Do you want to take the lead on this?"
Narrowing questions	A way to get a clear answer while also offering latitude in how that answer is framed including a potential rationale for the answer	"Who do you want to take the lead on this project?"
Open-ended questions	An opportunity to explore an issue in-depth	"What qualities do you think we need in a leader for this project?"

WHAT WE KNOW ABOUT QUESTIONS

Take a moment and consider the purpose of asking questions. When most people are asked what questions are for, they mention "getting answers." There is no doubt that questions are a good way of gathering information. Questions such as "How does artificial intelligence work?", "Do you have any allergies?", and "When is this due?" are all direct routes to acquiring information and saving time. But questions are far more versatile and have many more purposes than just learning things. Questions are also great for showing curiosity, demonstrating humility, building relationships, and provoking new thinking.

•   *Demonstrating interest.* Questions, it turns out, are signals to your conversational partners that you are interested in the topic and want to know more. When a coworker mentions to you that, before working in sales, they were a long-haul truck driver, you could answer with a conversation-killing, "oh." Or, you could express curiosity and ask questions such as "When was this?", "How long did you do that?", or "What was that like?" Each of these is a green light for the speaker to continue in greater depth.

• *Showing humility.* This aspect of asking questions is, perhaps, too often overlooked. Asking questions rather than sharing ideas or making recommendations can demonstrate humility. Questions such as "I wonder what needs to happen next?", "Who might be able to help?", or the powerful "What do you think we should do?" are helpful because they validate your conversational partners and offer them an opportunity to contribute.

• *Building relationships.* Asking a person about their experience, point of view, feelings, or opinions is a great way to express interest in them. This conversational investment suggests a commitment to the person and forms the seeds of a relationship. By contrast, people who ask very few questions and spend most of their time talking about themselves are generally less appealing as friends or colleagues.

• *Provoking new thinking.* Great questions can open a door to shifts in thinking. In fact, executive coaches, researchers, and inventors all share this approach to questioning. So-called "what-if" questions are examples of provocations, such as "What if we did it a different way?" or "What if it were possible?"

The varied functions of questions are, perhaps, why some people seem so hung up on asking "the right question." It is a sentiment expressed by the French philosopher Claude Lévi-Strauss, who reportedly said that a scientist is not a person who gives the right answers but who asks the right questions. In fact, a kind of mythology has sprung up around *the right question* as if it were a unicorn. This may, in fact, trace its roots to actual mythology; specifically, to the Oracle at Delphi. The Oracle only offered prophecies on a handful of nights a year and the line to ask questions was long. So, it seems, preparing the *right question* would have been important for pilgrims wanting to hear about their future.

In Radical Listening, the right question is contextual. It is the "most helpful question" in relation to the conversation. Are you asking a question to demonstrate that you do not know more than the speaker or are you asking one out of sheer curiosity? The main concern is "How can we use questions to best effect?", whether that is to enhance our ability to connect or to get the creative juices flowing. Any number of specific questions might work but being intentional about the use of certain types of questions is what gives them quality.

USE OF QUESTIONS IN RADICAL LISTENING

When we mentioned "certain types of questions" earlier, we were thinking about questions that can positively influence the conversation in particular ways. The premise of this book is that the *way* we listen to others can be enhanced by being clearer about our conversational intentions. Once our intention has been established, we can turn our attention to deploying the skills of listening, including questioning. In Radical Listening, there are five types of questions that are most helpful: supplementary, confirmatory, emphatic, celebratory, and future-focused. Each type is examined here (see Table 7.2 for a quick overview).

- *Supplementary questions* are ones that demonstrate our interest in the conversation by requesting additional information. At certain points in the conversation you can ask the speaker to elaborate on what they have just said. Supplementary questions should be used as a way of demonstrating interest and allowing the speaker to expand on topics that are relevant to the conversation. If this were a conversation instead of a book, you would be listening to

TABLE 7.2   Types of questions, based on their functions

Type	The purpose	An example
Supplementary	To draw out more detail about what has just been said	"What else was happening while you were dealing with this?"
Confirmatory	To highlight something positive in what has just been said	"So, you took matters into your own hands and resolved the situation?"
Emphatic	To show excitement	"All of this happened within ten minutes?"
Celebratory	To invite the speaker to celebrate their successes	"What were your most memorable highlights from that event?"
Future-focused	To encourage the speaker to turn their attention to the future	"How would you like things to be in the future?"

us—the authors—and might ask the supplementary question, "How would I know when to use a supplementary question?" (Good question! Read on!)

• *Confirmatory questions* are most useful when you want to emphasize or highlight something that your conversational partner has recently said. Again, this shows that you are interested in their topic while also being actively involved in highlighting key moments in the narrative. The purpose of this type of question is to linger on information or perspectives that may encourage the speaker by demonstrating your understanding and appreciation of what has been said. If you were listening to us now, you might ask us the following question: "So, the idea is to linger on something positive?"

• *Emphatic questions* aim to demonstrate high levels of engagement. Their purpose is to show our enthusiasm or commiseration about the narrative that is being shared. These questions need to be relatively short and punchy so that they do not disrupt the flow of the speaker. Their purpose is to amplify and signal excitement. If you were listening to us now, you might share your enthusiasm by asking us "When can we try this out?"

- *Celebratory questions* are a distinct form of inquiry. They are meant to point your conversational partner's attention toward praiseworthy aspects of their stories. The aim is to support them in identifying what they are most proud of in relation to their narrative or what went well. In practice, this means asking your conversational partner to tell you more about their strengths, skills, or successes. Because there can be both an instructional element and an appreciative element involved in celebratory questions, they are most appropriate to relationships where personal development is relevant. It feels appropriate for a manager to ask a supervisee, "What did you learn that helped you navigate this problem successfully?"

- *Future-focused questions* are important interventions in Radical Listening. Their aim is to draw attention toward positive futures. In the context of Radical Listening conversations, this allows the listener to understand and show interest in their conversational partner's motivation and goals. By asking about the future, you are likely to encourage your conversational partner to talk about a desired outcome. Often, this is a source of optimism and hope. If you were listening to us now, you might ask us "What impact do you hope this book will have?"

PUTTING IT INTO PRACTICE: EXPERIMENTING WITH QUESTIONS

The best way to become familiar with the types of questions that are helpful in Radical Listening conversations is to try them out in your own conversations. Let us be honest. Unless you are doing this already, it might come across as strange if you try all of these out on one person in one conversation. We recommend that you practice dropping these questions into conversations as appropriate. The important thing for this practice is to decide which of these you would like to experiment with *prior* to the conversation. For now, work one or two into the conversation and then take note of how your conversational partner responds. In this case, and with all the skills covered in this book, authenticity and genuineness are foundational. These are not tricks to manipulate others—they are simply ways of being explicit about your interest in your conversational partner and the topics that they discuss.

TYPES OF QUESTIONS THAT INTERFERE WITH RADICAL LISTENING

There is an experience that psychologists call the "I knew it all along" phenomenon.[1] The hindsight bias is particularly common when people look back at events, such as sports tournaments, product launches, or political elections. Once the events have concluded and it is easy to see the factors that determined the outcomes, people think that they could easily have predicted them from the outset. Similarly, when people learn about Radical Listening, they sometimes believe that they already know all about questions. "I've been using supplementary and emphatic questions my whole life," they might say.

Although it is undoubtedly true that you naturally use many of these question types effectively, most people have also acquired some bad habits over time. Here, we review the types of questions that should be *avoided* to provide the best experience for your conversational partners. These include cluster questions, ramblers, random questions, Trojan horses, and rhetorical questions (see Table 7.3).

- *Cluster questions.* This term refers to asking multiple questions back-to-back. They are often the result of someone trying to

TABLE 7.3 Types of questions to avoid

Type	The issue	An example
The cluster question	Multiple questions asked consecutively	How is the project going? It's not very different from the one we did last year, right? Is that affecting the team's morale?
The rambler	The question itself is poorly formed and lacks focus	So, I have a question for you. It's more of an observation than a question, maybe. But how can we address the complaint of our client—maybe 'complaint' is too strong a word—but you know what I mean—how do we address the client's concerns without upsetting the team who have been working on this project for two years—they're not going to take it well, are they?
The random question	The question is not related to what the speaker is saying	On a completely different topic, did we ever respond to that request from head office?
The Trojan horse	The question is just a way of giving advice	How about we take some time to reflect on today's experience and then reconvene in the morning?
The rhetorical question	The question is used to make a point rather than solicit a response	What is the point of us sharing our views if they are just going to ignore what we say?

formulate progressively better questions even as they are speaking. They will ask one question, think of better ones, and then pose those immediately without giving their conversational partner a chance to respond to the first. For example, a person might ask you, "How was your trip to London? What did you do? Did you visit Buckingham Palace?" On the receiving end, the cluster question is confusing, leaving the respondent with doubts about which of the questions to address. Cluster questions create a conversational logjam, or they force the speaker to make tough choices and to ignore some of the listener's questions. The antidote to this is to slow down. Feel free to take your time and land on a single, helpful question. Because what would happen if you did not? How would it affect others? Who would it affect? What might it say about your ability to listen? How would others see you?

•   *The rambler.* This may be the most frustrating type of question that we will discuss here. It is a question that lacks clarity and seems to meander even as it is being asked. The rambler occurs when the person asking the question seems to be formatting it as they are speaking (almost like they are thinking aloud). It can be complicated by traditional notions of active listening, in which listeners feel obliged to repeat whole swathes of what the speaker has just said. For example, someone posing a rambler might say, "So, Preeti, it sounds like you are feeling a little sidelined on this project due, in part, to your lack of seniority and I guess what I am wondering, in thinking about the ways that seniority might or might not be a factor in the way that we allocate roles on projects, is whether this hints at something institutional that we need to change, or maybe if it is just a one-off event, or if this is uniquely related to your own experience." We have all been on the receiving end of ramblers and they can be difficult to track, confusing, and can sap energy from the conversation. One antidote to rambling questions is to drop the preamble entirely: ditch all the so-called active listening elements in which you repeat what the person has just said. Trust, instead, that acknowledging and questioning, themselves, are demonstrations of active (even radical!) listening. Having said that, to be clear, it seems like the most important point is that a person does not have to repeat what was just said in order to be a terrific listener and if they dropped that long preamble, how do you think it might help the question-asking process?

•   *Random questions.* Random questions are those that feel irrelevant. For example, if a person tells their coworker, "I bumped into Tanya at the gym last night" and the coworker responds, "Really? What kind of shoes was she wearing?" The question is jarring because the speaker is not able to see how it is important to the topic or helps the flow of the conversation. Even when it makes sense to the person asking the question, its seemingly random nature can lead to the conversational partner feeling as if they are not being listened to. In this example, it might be that the listener saw that Tanya left her workout shoes by her desk and was curious about what she was wearing. As is common with random questions, it dismisses the speaker's story in favor of a personal curiosity. Rather than doing anything that could undermine rapport, it is usually better to hold the question for another conversation. Having said that, what are the cultural norms related to punctuality where you live?

•   *The Trojan horse.* We are all guilty of occasionally disguising our advice as a question. For example, "Have you ever thought about seeing a therapist who specializes in anger management?" is not an idle curiosity. Nor will the person hearing this question think so. Trojan horse questions are to be avoided because they can be manipulative and, well, too advice-y. The antidote to this approach— if you do have a piece of advice or a suggestion—is to offer it explicitly. For example, it is more transparent to say "I think that you should seek legal advice before handing in your notice" rather than present concealed advice such as "Do you know anyone who has sought legal advice before handing in their notice?" When you ask questions, they should be genuine. Most often, Trojan horse questions are asked unintentionally when we are trying to guide a person's thinking without telling them what they should do. How might you create time to reflect on your use of questions to avoid Trojan horse questions when you are talking to others?

•   *The rhetorical question.* This has all the characteristics of a question but, perversely, is not really intended to be answered. Its main purpose is to make a point. For example, asking "Do you want to get fired from your job?" is generally a commentary on workplace performance and less an inquiry into a person's intention to remain employed. Rhetorical questions are effective in political speeches, dramas, and debates, but not helpful as a way of building connection or demonstrating interest in your conversational partner. For this reason, rhetorical questions should be avoided when engaging in Radical Listening. After all, who wants to go into a conversation expecting a dialogue and end up being on the receiving end of a monologue?

Now you understand that there are certain types of questions to avoid. Instead, to be a great listener, you should ask other types of questions. Namely, those that are intentional. Therefore, the answer to the question, "How would I know when to use a supplementary question?" will be related to what will lead to the listener feeling that they have been heard.

Conversations are dynamic, like a tennis match or the relationship between musicians and their audiences. In conversation, everyone is involved. Speakers and listeners take turns and even the listening side of the discussion is highly active and involved. When listeners ask questions to fill their own curiosity, or to steer the conversation to a topic that is more interesting to them, or to offer advice when it is not asked for, they are not engaged in Radical Listening.

HOW SMALL CAN A QUESTION BE?

So far, we have made the case for the use of questions to *enhance* the way that we listen to others and consider which types of questions might help or hinder that effort. Now, we will turn our attention to more subtle ways of bringing questions into your Radical Listening conversations. Namely, by using *micro-questions*. These can be highly effective because they are also the least intrusive. Micro-questions are questions that are stripped down to their most essential parts. They are often only a single word or two. Examples include such questions such as "Oh?", "Really?", "That often?", "What now?", and "How come?" These tiny questions can provide much of the value of their bigger linguistic siblings.

In fact, micro-questions have several advantages. First, they demonstrate engagement without being intrusive. When you ask "That was you?" or "Really?" or "When?" you are calling for the speaker to keep speaking without derailing them. This is especially helpful in instances in which the speaker is brainstorming, telling a funny or engaging story, or is teaching something. The micro-question signals that the listener is paying attention and invites the speaker to elaborate. In addition, micro-questions typically change the pace of a conversation. The switch between the role of speaker and that of listener is so quick that it is hardly noticeable—another advantage of these tiny inquiries.

What is even smaller than a micro-question? You might be tempted to say "a nano-question," but the answer we are looking for here is "silence." Sometimes silence from the listener can act as a question. Excellent listeners can convey skepticism through silence as if they were asking the question, "What is the evidence for that?" They can also signal interest with silence, as if they were asking "Can you say more about that?" This can be helpful when, although the speaker has paused, they might have more to say. For example, when a person says, "There is just no way back from this. I cannot see how we fix this at all," they might be doing more than just communicating worry and frustration. They might be trying to see a way to fix the problem. Rather than jumping in with an immediate question, a short pause might give them the room they need to explore further. Silence, in this case, is a stand-in for questions like "What else?" The use of a silence in conversations is like "passing" on your turn. By not saying anything, you are also indicating that it is still your conversational partner's turn to speak.

**PUTTING IT INTO PRACTICE: HOW SMALL CAN
A CONVERSATION BE?**

Just for fun, have a conversation by trying to rely on the most minimal aspects of communication: facial expressions, silence, and microquestions. See what happens when you limit yourself to minimal interactions, repeating short phrases, or asking the bare minimum. We think you might be surprised with the results. We recommend starting with close friends or family members!

SUMMARY

Far from getting in the way of Radical Listening, the judicious use of questions can demonstrate your commitment to a conversation, increase the energy of the interaction, and strengthen the rapport between you and your conversational partner. Essentially, Radical Listening depends on a clear intention and commitment from you to be a good conversational partner. This means that you must do more than listen attentively. You need to become an active participant in the conversation. The use of questions provides you with a practical and engaging way of doing so.

QUESTIONS

1. Do you have a favorite question? What about it appeals to you?
2. Do you have a question that you dislike being asked? What about the question rubs you the wrong way?
3. How might you use the various types of questions, such as confirmatory or emphatic, to improve your listening and communication?

CHAPTER EIGHT

INTERJECTING

Few places are more centered around the idea of high-quality listening than the symphony. Around the world, some of the most beautiful and acoustically advanced spaces are those that are home to urban orchestras. On a Tuesday evening, in January 2012, the famed New York Philharmonic was making its way through the slow strings of the end of Mahler's Symphony No. 9 when it was interrupted.[1] From the pocket of an audience member, the familiar marimba ringtone called out. The conductor motioned for the players to stop and a couple of thousand people sat and listened to the woody chiming as the phone rang over and over before finally going to voicemail. In symphony circles, it was an event so big that it was covered by the New York Times, the Daily Mail, and CNN. Concertgoers demanded that the culprit be fined or prohibited from attending future performances. They did so because people find interruptions to be one of the main obstacles to listening.

Today, the average person lives into their late seventies. This means that if you had only a single conversation a day, you would have about 28,000 conversations in your lifetime. That is why there are such well-established rules about how to speak and how to listen. Despite some cultural variation, most people intuitively understand that being a good listener means that you follow some basic tenets: take turns to speak, pay attention, and listen in relative silence. Interruptions, by definition, break the "take turns to speak" guideline and so it is no wonder that people so often find this behavior offensive.

Despite our general disapproval of interruptions, we sometimes seem surprisingly willing to accept them. We withstand interruptions regularly, and even occasionally appreciate them. For example, an airline captain will break into your movie or conversation to provide you with information. The government uses the Child Rescue Alert (United Kingdom) or AMBER Alert (United States) to interrupt your texting with urgent messages about a crime. Television programs are interrupted by commercials and live sporting and arts events are interrupted by an intermission. Your pet might interrupt your dinner or leisure reading to be fed or let outside. Coworkers interrupt your concentration when their messages pop up in your internal messaging app. The list goes on. In each case, these might seem like a mild irritant but, just as often, we perceive them as important, justified, and sometimes even welcome breaks.

It might seem easy to dismiss these examples. After all, they are not—strictly speaking—interruptions of live conversations. There seems, at first blush, to be a qualitative difference between a general interruption such as a public service announcement and a person talking over you in a conversation. It is easy to see the rationale for the former—to provide important information—whereas our best guess for the latter boils down to not following the basic rules of conversation. Societally, we would consider this rude.

In this chapter, we offer the possibility that there is more to interrupting than meets the ear. To help make the case for this, we will refer to it as interjecting (and occasionally as interrupting). Even the word interjecting sounds more polite and acceptable than its alternative. This is more than whitewashing or wordplay, however. As counterintuitive as it sounds, interjection is a vital part of listening. Skillful interjection is one of the most engaged forms of Radical Listening.

THE ANATOMY OF A CONVERSATION

For the past fifty years, linguists have studied conversational interactions. For the most part, they are curious about how people use speech to convey meaning, establish and maintain rapport, and express themselves. This large program of research has led, inevitably, to the study of interruptions in conversations. Researchers have found mixed evidence for some of the phenomena about which you have a strong intuition. For example, some studies reveal that women interrupt at higher rates and other studies point to men as more frequent interrupters.[2] Similarly, people of higher social status, such as judges or doctors, might be more likely to interrupt, but some studies suggest that patients interrupt doctors more than the other way around.[3] Finally, some studies have found interruptions to be cooperative and helpful![4]

What, exactly, are these scientists looking at when they identify an interruption? A simple, non-emotive way to understand interruptions is that they are "overlapping speech." That is, any time that two people speak simultaneously, an interruption happens. The reason this is interesting is that it suggests that you interrupt constantly! Every time you say, "mmm-hmmm" or "yeah" or "no way" you interrupt the speaker. These small interjections typically do not feel like interruptions, though. Not to the interrupter and not even to the speaker.

This raises the question of whether there are types of interruptions. It seems like there must be some difference between saying "mmm hmmm" and barging into a person's story with an anecdote of your own. We argue that, indeed, there are many distinct flavors of interruption. These include:

- *Asides.* This occurs when one person is talking and two or more others have a side conversation. Imagine, for example, a presentation by a salesperson. While the presenter is speaking one person turns to their seatmate and whispers "What did she just say?" or "This is really nothing new. We've known about this trend for ages."
- *Minimal encouragers.* As the name suggests, these are signals to a speaker that the listener understands and wants the speaker to continue. They are typically small—perhaps only a word or two—and examples include "uh huh," "yes," "go on," and "mmmm."
- *Humor.* Making jokes and being playful is a unique form of interjection. It relies on timing and offers a lighthearted, and often unexpected response where none is required. For instance, a speaker might introduce a story by saying "guess what." In this case, the speaker is not necessarily soliciting a guess. Instead, they are signaling that some news or information is to follow. Even so, a quick-witted listener might use the opportunity for a funny interjection such as offering the guess, "You are about to buy me lunch?"
- *Alerts.* This is, perhaps, a slightly less common but still familiar form of interjection. In this case, a listener interrupts a speaker to alert them to a problem. For example, they might say "You shouldn't say that so loud. He is sitting at the table behind you," or "Before you get too deep into this, I think your basic math has an error."
- *Stealing the podium.* This is the classic interruption that is so widely considered offensive. Here, the listener does not wait for their turn to speak and, instead, just starts speaking over the previous speaker. This can happen because of enthusiasm for the topic, as an exercise of social power, to correct or explain, or because of poor social skills.
- *Taking the microphone.* This is the most extreme form of interruption. It is intended to prevent another person from speaking or

sharing their perspectives. This is a form of censorship and it is often imposed by force.

This is only a partial list and there are many others. These interjections differ on several dimensions. First, they differ from one another in magnitude. That is, some are large and some are relatively small. They also differ in politeness, with some being considered polite and others perceived as rude (see Figure 8.1).

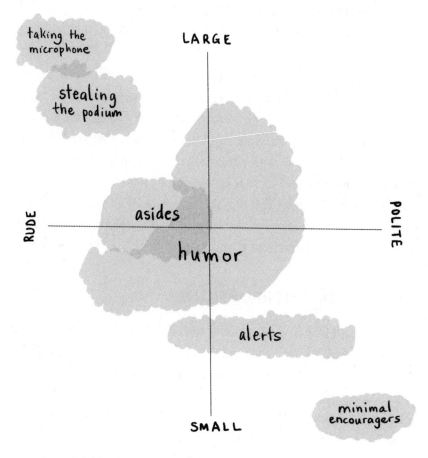

FIGURE 8.1 Understanding types of interruptions
Source: Developed by the authors

Perhaps the most important thing to understand, where the politeness or rudeness of interjecting is concerned, is how it relates to turn-taking in a conversation. It is common to understand a conversation as a series of turns to speak much in the same way as a tennis match is made of turns to hit the ball. If, however, one player threw an extra ball on the court and hit it, this would be seen as a serious breach of rules. Where conversation is concerned, most interruptions are interjections—overlapping speech that steals the turn to speak but then immediately returns it to the original speaker. When you insert a funny comment, offer a helpful correction, or ask for clarification, you typically do so quickly and then fall back into listening mode.

This conversational dance is so well understood that speakers are often not aware that the interjection is actually an interruption at all. The late David Peterson, who ran coaching at Google for about a decade, experimented with interruptions in his coaching sessions.[5] He was curious to see how many times in a row he could interrupt with a statement or question before it irritated his clients. His answer was multiple times! In a row! This may be because quick comments or questions are seen as (a) relevant and helpful to the conversation, and (b) only momentary distractions that are quickly replaced by listening.

A WORLD OF INTERRUPTIONS

To understand how to distinguish between non-offensive interjections and rude interruptions, we should turn to culture. When people think of culture, they often envision the most visible aspects of culture: dress, cuisine, religious imagery, or language. Although each of these is a manifestation of culture, it is a more complicated phenomenon than these examples suggest. One simple way to understand culture is that it is a set of norms that a person learns from others about how to feel, think, interact, and communicate. Cultural norms inform—to name just a few examples—how people express emotions, how they see themselves in a social hierarchy, how they think about punctuality, and how they believe a conversation should flow. Cultures around the world have created very specific norms where speaking and conversation are concerned.

People from some cultures believe in making small talk such as asking about family before getting to important business. People from other cultures, such as the Amish or some Inuit groups, feel comfortable sitting together in silence even for long periods at a stretch. Still others differ in the roundabout way they like to address topics. Erin Meyer, professor of management at INSEAD business school, offers an example of this last point.[6] She argues that when people make evaluations of others—such as giving feedback on job performance—cultures differ in their prescription for how direct or indirect this feedback should be. Dutch people, for instance, have a reputation for being blunt. Within the context of Dutch culture, their straightforward manner is viewed as direct and honest. For outsiders, however, being told that one is "inflexible" or "slow to pick up on things" can be a slap in the face. By contrast, Americans—known for their upbeat attitudes—tend to wrap negative feedback within a pretty gauze of praise. This is so common in the United States that there is something known as a "feedback sandwich" in which a person offers a compliment, then a negative criticism, and then another compliment.

You can see attitudes about communication in the proverbs of a language. For example, one Japanese saying translates to, "If the bird had not sung it would not have been shot." This suggests that, in Japanese culture, people might be cautious about speaking up. By contrast, Americans believe that "the squeaky wheel gets the grease," a proverb that encourages speaking up. The Akan people of Ghana have a proverb that translates to, "the wise is spoken in proverbs, not in plain language," suggesting that one should be cautious about being too direct in one's speech.

You might imagine that the same cultural trends that give rise to Dutch or Inuit or Canadian or Japanese or Akan conversational norms also govern the way interruptions are perceived. The linguist Deborah Tannen has researched the culture of interruption in some small but interesting studies.[7] For example, she examined the conversational style of New Yorkers. The stereotype of New Yorkers is that they speak with a strong accent, speak rapidly, and can come across as conversationally pushy. Tannen recorded the conversation of people attending an American Thanksgiving holiday dinner; some were New Yorkers, some were Californians, and one was from London. She evaluated their speaking style in terms of pacing, topic of discussion, storytelling, and other features. Tannen arrived at several interesting conclusions as a result:

1.   *Differing interpretations of simultaneous speech.* The New Yorkers were more likely than the others to speak along with the speaker. Imagine, for example, a speaker offering a conversational opening such as "So, I just finished reading *War and Peace.*" And then, while the speaker starts describing their experience of the novel, the listener says "Oh, Tolstoy. He's one of my favorites. Especially Anna Karenina." According to Tannen, this would be a show of active and engaged listening and not considered at all rude by New York standards. By contrast, the other party attendees considered it an interruption and, as a consequence, quit speaking. As soon as they quit speaking the interjection, therefore, did become an actual interruption.

2.   *Differing perceptions of pauses in conversation.* The New Yorkers looked for tiny pauses in the conversation and viewed these as openings to jump in. When a speaker stopped to consider a word, catch their breath, or hold for dramatic impact, it signaled the end of the turn to speak to the New Yorkers. By contrast, the others waited for long pauses, which often never came, and so had a harder time inserting themselves into the conversation.

Tannen's study also illustrates an important element of listening: the consequences of a collision between two distinct conversational cultures. Part of Radical Listening, then—and especially the part that involves interjection—is predicated on some amount of cultural intelligence. It is crucial to understand a few important factors: whether the person you are speaking with has a high or low tolerance for overlapping speech; how comfortable they are with conversational silence; their preferred pace of speech; and how they use pauses. This cultural acumen is sometimes called "code-switching."

Code-switching is the modifying of language and behavior in ways that make them more culturally appropriate and effective. For example, in some cultures, it is customary to bow as a sign of respect. In others, people might put their palms together to greet one another. Shaking hands is another culturally specific way of greeting people. You might choose to maintain more silence in some cultures and offer more enthusiastic disagreement in others. It is worth noting that code-switching often means accommodating another person's communication style. For instance, Tannen tells a story about how, in conversations with a friend, she mentally counts to seven before speaking in the hope that this long pause gives her companion ample opportunity to enter the conversation.[8]

The alternative to simply bending yourself to whatever local rules apply to a conversation is to engineer a culture in which interjections are helpful and positive but in which interruptions can be rude and are kept to a minimum. This is especially possible in a work team or other small group that has relatively strong control over its own norms. Establishing a basis for interjection as a form of enthusiastic listening can be as simple as being transparent about what you are doing. When group members understand the various types of simultaneous speech and appreciate how some are related to good listening they become much more accepting of the occasional interjection.

RADICAL LISTENING: INTERJECTION

If you were to ask, "How is Radical Listening different from standard notions of listening—or even from active listening?" the answer is to be found, in part, in interjection. Some academics, such as the Japanese linguist Kumiko Murata, suggest that interruptions can be categorized into those that are "intrusive" (harmful to the flow of a conversation) and those that are "cooperative" (helpful to the flow of a conversation).[9] This is the first hint that some interruptions are, in fact, beneficial. For example, imagine a listener jumping in to clarify a confusing point. This is not only polite but is also necessary to help the conversationalists understand one another and to proceed effectively. We can reverse engineer interruptions to see what types of comments or questions might fall into the helpful and unhelpful categories (see Table 8.1).

Assuming we have addressed the question of "How should I interject in ways that are helpful?" there is still the question of, "When should I interject in ways that are helpful?" In the decades that we—the authors of this book—have been coaches, we have paid close attention to the timing of interjections. Although this might not be a comprehensive list, we have identified three distinct moments that call for interjection.[10]

1. *Procedural interjections.* These are especially relevant to professional conversations such as a diagnostic doctor's visit, a meeting with a financial adviser, or visiting a psychotherapist. Procedural interjections are those that are offered by whoever is considered the facilitator of the conversation. They are aimed at the procedural aspects of the conversation: timekeeping, clarifying, or "planting seeds" for later work. Of these, time-related interjections are, perhaps, the most common. An example of this would be when a financial advisor interrupts to say, "I note that we have ten minutes left and I want to make certain that you get everything you came in for. Is there anything we have

TABLE 8.1 Helpful and unhelpful interruptions

Intrusive interruptions (unhelpful to the flow of the conversation)	Cooperative interruptions (helpful to the conversational participants)
Diversion: Offering personal stories or other information that is not relevant or is only partially relevant to the conversation	*Clarification*: Asking for more information so that you or others in the conversation can better understand or follow what is being said
Disagreement: Derailing or cutting short the speaker by offering disagreement, opposing facts, or a counteroffer	*Agreement*: Quick words, gestures, or sounds that signal agreement and which encourage the speaker to continue
Stealing the podium: Grabbing the turn to speak and holding on to it. This is sometimes done as a power play and sometimes by a lack of social awareness. It is almost always considered rude	*Assistance*: Listeners often supply a missing word, piece of information, or clarification to the speaker to help them more effectively communicate information
Taking the microphone: Preventing someone from having a voice. This is political and would definitely be considered highly intrusive	*Rallying*: When listeners seek to rally support for the speaker by supporting the perspective that is being presented or the right of the person to voice their opinion (e.g., "preach" or "you go girl")

not yet covered that you would like to?" These count as interruptions because they often require the listener to step in while the speaker is talking. This is particularly true if the conversation has turned to small talk or humor. In our experience, speakers are highly tolerant of procedural interjections because there is a clear and transparent rationale for them.

2. *Emphatic interjections.* These occur when the speaker says something really important or noteworthy—a manager revealing that a team surpassed all benchmarks for the quarter, a colleague explaining that they have never given a presentation before such a large group, or a new hire saying that they noticed a critical problem in the onboarding process. In each of these cases, it can be important to pounce on the

moment rather than let it slip by out of a sense of politeness. In fact, it can seem rude to let someone tell a long story only to respond by saying, "I'd like to go back and address something you said four minutes ago. . . ." Emphatic interjections are those that, as the name implies, seek to emphasize what is being said and to highlight it as important. In coaching, for instance, a coach might cut off a client mid-sentence to ask, "Did you hear what you just said?" Doing so offers the possibility of raising self-awareness in the client and of addressing a particular statement while it is still "emotionally hot." Emphatic interjections tend to be relatively quick. They are often a single question or a short command, such as "Tell me more," or a strong reaction such as "Wow" or "I had no idea" or "Congratulations!"

3. *Strategic interjections.* These are, perhaps, the least commonly occurring and most highly targeted form of interruption. Strategic interjections are offered with a very specific and well-intentioned conversational goal in mind. For instance, a listener might interject a quick, humorous comment to dispel tension in a conversation that is heating up emotionally. Another example can be found in alerting a speaker to their surroundings. For instance, imagine planning a surprise retirement party for a colleague but the listener interrupts to say "Here she comes" so that the speaker understands to stop talking about that topic. Rallying support for the speaker by telling others that she is "on fire" is one way of providing active support. As with the other forms of interjection, strategic interruptions are typically very quick and their rationale is readily apparent to the speaker.

SUMMARY

Radical Listening asks you to reconsider your notions of interrupting. Although everyone knows it is generally considered rude, we should also acknowledge that it can sometimes be helpful. Being able to determine when and how to interject is, perhaps, the most engaged and active form of listening. This skill requires a wide range of social intelligences. First, it involves being aware of cultural differences in speaking and listening. It also means accommodating styles of speech by revising how you perceive pauses, how you use silence, and how much time you allow before speaking. More than anything, effective interjection is fast. Although it is technically an interruption in that it temporarily steals the limelight, it is more acceptable because it does so with social connection in mind and it returns the podium to the speaker almost immediately.

When done well, interjection conveys enthusiasm for the conversation and support for the speaker. It is summed up nicely by Judith Martin, who has spent decades writing an etiquette column. Martin advocates a highly engaged view of listening. She writes: "If you are, in fact, a practiced 'good listener' you have not been traveling through life in silence. You have been asking questions, inserting relevant information, and providing commentary. . . . A good listener is not someone who has to be checked every now and then by the speaker to see if he or she is awake."[11]

QUESTIONS

1. What are your own attitudes about interruption? How permissible versus rude do you consider it?
2. When you think about overlapping speech, such as saying "mmmhmm" or "yeah," how rude do you think this is? What do you think makes it feel different than other forms of interruption? What does this tell you about listening?
3. How will you experiment with quick interjections that have the potential to improve your conversations?

PART FOUR

· · · · ● ● ● ● ● ● ● ● · · ·

THE LISTENING CONTEXT

Listening is not simply a part of communication between people. It is a skill that is linked to the environment. Listening at a rock concert is qualitatively different than listening in a board meeting. Both of these are distinct from listening to the crunch of leaves under our feet in the forest. The environment influences every aspect of listening— what we listen to, what we listen for, and how easy it is to listen. Reducing background noise and other distractions can make listening easier and more effective.

In the earlier sections of this book, we presented a framework for Radical Listening and devoted chapters to each of its specific parts. In this section, we build on these ideas by recognizing the fact that each listening skill will manifest differently depending on context. If the earlier sections represent "Radical Listening 101," then this section is the advanced course. These chapters recognize that the simple skills of listening become increasingly complex when we shift from the pages of a book to real-world situations.

Here, we discuss the context of culture as a specific listening environment. There are countless books and articles written on cross-cultural communication and we attempt to create a primer here with a specific focus on listening across cultures. We begin with a definition and history of culture and link this to the psychological dimensions of culture such as identity and the expression of emotion. Then, we drill down on the specific aspects of culture that are tied to listening, such as paying attention to nonverbal behavior, understanding norms for conflict, and noticing the ways that social hierarchy affects interactions.

Radical Listening concludes with a final chapter about creating fertile ground for high-quality conversations and interactions—in groups, organizations, and societies. Here, we share some guidelines for creating ideal environments for Radical Listening conversations and a few thoughts about why listening is now more important than ever.

CHAPTER NINE

LISTENING ACROSS CULTURES

For decades, Braniff International Airways operated in the United States and nearby nations. It was especially famous for its marketing campaigns, which featured celebrities and artists flying on its planes. It became well-known for operating the supersonic Concorde service in concert with partner European carriers. It was also famous for an error in translation in a Latin American radio ad. In English, the advertisement encouraged potential passengers to "fly in leather;" a nod to its non-fabric seats. In the Spanish translation, however, "in leather" is also slang for naked. The campaign suggested that the skies are even friendlier than we might have thought!

There are dozens of famous (or notorious) examples of mistranslations in business and politics. Some of these are urban myths whereas others are verified. Sometimes, these "lost in translation" moments are humorous, as in the case of flying naked. Other times, they are problematic. One example is the US marketing campaign "Got Milk?" which successfully promoted drinking milk by showcasing celebrities with a "milk mustache." In South America, however, the catchphrase was seen as an explicit reference to breastfeeding rather than a cheeky catchphrase related to a breakfast item. In this context, "got milk" came across as an overt challenge to people who did not always have access to formula (powdered milk) and it felt harsh. Wisely, the advertisers modified the campaign for that market. In any case, translation is only one example of the complexities of cross-cultural communication.

It is easy to think that Radical Listening is a singular concept. This entire book is organized around a simple framework: It contains six discrete listening skills, three of which are internal and three of which are behavioral. In a global context, however, Radical Listening is less "by the book" than one might think. The very definitions of "quiet" and "interjecting" differ from culture to culture. The way that people "acknowledge" and "question" vary from place to place. As stand-alone skills, they are easy to understand and appear simple to use. In the real world, however, social interactions can be complicated. Here, we take the general precepts of Radical Listening and discuss them with more cultural nuance. To do so, we offer a crash course in culture so that you can better understand its influence on communication.

A NOTE ON DISCUSSING CULTURE

You would think that discussing societal differences would be straightforward. It does not feel too controversial to mention that women in India often wear *saris* or that Canadians have a unique love for the band *The Tragically Hip*, or that Europeans take soccer (football) pretty seriously. Even so, there is a hint of generalizing in such statements. Not all women in India wear saris, not all Canadians are fans of the band, and there are Europeans who do not care about sports at all.

Once we shift from the visible artifacts of culture—such as dress, language, and cuisine—and start discussing the psychological aspects of culture—what people believe, how they think, and how they communicate—the problem gets even worse. At best, it can feel like well-intentioned stereotyping and, at worst, like open prejudice, eth-nocentrism, or racism. Making cultural generalities rubs against modern sensibilities regarding inclusion and respect for diversity. Saying, for instance, "Jamaicans have historically performed well in Olympic sprinting events" feels like accurate reporting, whereas "Chinese people eat with chopsticks" lands less well.

The root of the issue is not the assumed sensitivities of modern readers but the fact that any discussion of culture deals with generalities. This is a problem that social scientists have confronted for decades. The quantitative results of studies are averages, and so a discussion of cultural research is often about trends rather than a description of every individual within a society. Researchers would be the first to acknowledge that, of course, there is variation within cultural groups.

It is also worth noting the counterexamples; that there are many instances in which you are likely comfortable with generalizations associated with social categories. You probably do not mind that students often receive discounts even though some students are wealthy. You likely do not object to policies that allow less strict security screening for airplane passengers over seventy-five years old even though an older adult could pose a threat. You might not even mind someone making the point that women are generally paid less than men even though this is not true in every case. One solution, then, is to use generalities to guide discussion without foreclosing on the idea that they accurately represent every single member of a group.

The field of clinical psychology offers one possible way of dealing with this thread-the-needle phenomenon: wanting to be informed by cultural trends, on the one hand, while also respecting the unique individual on the other hand. In the 1990s, two clinical psychologists advocated an approach to psychotherapy that they called the "local clinical scientist" model.[1] Here is how it works: A therapist knows some general things about, say, depression. The therapist knows the most common causes and symptoms of depression and even how these vary across age and culture. But then, a unique person sits in the chair across from them. The therapist gauges the extent to which this person is "typical" of their general knowledge about depression. That is, to what degree does this person represent the "average" or to what degree do they diverge from it? In doing so, the therapist balances the general with the unique.

We can do the same with culture. We understand, for instance, that hospitality is generally an important concept in the Middle East. If a salesperson visits Beirut on a business trip, they might reasonably assume that their host will show them around and invite them to dinner. If the host suggests, instead, that the salesperson eat room service alone in a hotel room then these assumptions would have to be revised, at least as they relate to the host. In this way, knowledge of culture acts like a guiding script and you can mentally revise this script based on the interaction at hand. This is why understanding cultural scripts and trends can be so critical to advanced Radical Listening. These are conversational tendencies that we might *listen for (pay attention to)* to get more out of our interactions.

A BRIEF DEFINITION OF CULTURE

What is culture? It turns out that there are multiple ways to view this phenomenon.[2] First, there is the idea that culture is something that is cultivated. In this instance, there is a high overlap between the concept of social class and that of culture. A "cultured person," by this line of reasoning, is one who has developed a taste for high culture, such as an appreciation of art, travel, and classical literature.

Another way to think about culture is as a way of life that is learned. This is, perhaps, the most common understanding of culture. It can be seen in the various languages, clothing choices, and religions of people around the world. In some cultures, for example, the way of life is to shake hands when you greet someone and, in other cultures, it is more common to press one's hands together in a prayer position or place a hand over one's heart. The length of lunch breaks (if any), the age of retirement (if it exists), and which side of the road people drive on are all examples of this form of culture.

The final way to understand culture is to see it as shared learning. Whether absorbed through observation, taught by parents, or learned at school, culture—in this sense—is a shared way of understanding the world and how it works. Often, the cultural messages here are so powerful that it is not always obvious that there are alternatives. For instance, the concept of "middle age" does not exist in all cultures. What seems normal for a Canadian—the idea of a midlife crisis—is completely foreign to a Maasai living in Kenya. Similarly, the idea that attaining public success, high status, and advanced education are taken-for-granted aspirations in some cultures, whereas they are less important in others.

Seeing culture in these distinct ways is not a trivial matter. Each offers information about what a conversational partner might value or insights that might help you better interpret their interaction style. These approaches to culture offer targets for noticing and acknowledging, for questions, and provide clues about how best to interject. They provide a roadmap for conversational etiquette and norms for communication, and can therefore enhance listening.

THE PSYCHOLOGICAL CONSEQUENCES OF CULTURE

Culture exists in groups of all sizes whether that is a sales team, a hospital in London, or the nation of Australia. At the societal level, acculturation tends to emphasize either the importance of the group or the importance of the individual. Does this matter? You bet. These turn out to be more than geographical preferences. The degree to which a person is acculturated in an individualist or collectivist society

TABLE 9.1 Individualism and collectivism

	Individualism	Collectivism
View of self	Individual Reflects on and expresses personal opinions and feelings Prioritizes personal goals Behavior is based on personality	Part of a group Reflects more on norms and appropriateness Prioritizes group goals Behavior is based on personality and situation
View of personal control	People can control situations and outcomes, at least in part Success is a product of effort Feelings and other states are a choice	People can adapt to situations Success is a product of effort, connections, and fortune Situations and states happen; they are not a choice
How attention is focused	Likely to notice individual objects Likely to notice distinct objects	Likely to notice context Likely to notice background objects
How objects are clustered	Likely to group objects by category	Likely to group objects by their relation to one another

affects the way that people see themselves, understand the limits of their personal control, and even shapes the ways that they pay attention and think (see Table 9.1). Specifically:

1. *Their view of the self.*[3] Individualists are likely to see themselves as an independent unit. They are the protagonists in the story of their lives. They have their own feelings, opinions, and memories. They have a right to pursue their own goals and dreams and will do so even if these aspirations come in conflict with the desires of their group. They see themselves in terms of stable personality traits and are likely to see others as relatively stable and predictable in behavior. By contrast, collectivists are likely to see themselves as part of a larger group. They are one member of the cast in the play of life. Sure, they have their

own preferences, but they are more likely to put those on the back burner if they come into conflict with the goals of the group. They see their behavior as resulting not from personality or situational influences but from a combination of the two. They are more tolerant of inconsistent behavior because they view it as stemming from situational influences.

2. *Their view of personal control.*[4] Individualists are likely to see themselves as agents of change. They see the world as something that they can control or at least influence. Similarly, they are likely to attribute the behavior of others as a conscious attempt to exert influence or control. By contrast, collectivists are likely to see themselves as ensconced in situations. They are more likely to emphasize adapting to a situation rather than attempting to control or change it.

3. *How they focus their attention.*[5] Imagine looking at a video of an aquatic scene—several types of fish, a sea fan, a shell, some bubbles, and some rocks. Researchers showed participants exactly such a scene and then asked what they had noticed. Results revealed that individualists are more likely to notice objects. There were, for instance, four fish. They attend to what is distinct. By contrast, collectivists are more likely to attend to context. Whereas individualists noticed the fish— presumably the stars of the show in their minds—their collectivist counterparts were more likely to notice the sea fan or other background details. In fact, they made 60 percent more references to background information. What's more, the collectivists were more likely to comment on the entire tableau, such as saying "it looks like a pond" or "it looks like a fish tank."

4. *How they cluster objects together.*[6] Related to the way people focus their attention, people are also likely to cluster objects based on cultural leanings. Specifically, individualists are likely to group objects by category. They might respond to the aquatic tableau described earlier by saying "There were four fish" or "There were two sea fans." The alternative, more likely to be showcased by their collectivist

counterparts, is to see objects in relation to one another. For example, these research participants might say "Three fish were facing one direction while the fourth was facing the opposite direction," or "The largest fish was in front of a sea fan." This is more than laboratory studies on fish; it is a description of what people notice and how they interpret relationships between things. In conversation, for instance, one person might be sensitive to the mention of the contribution of team members while another person pays closer attention to the description of the project. Both are hearing the same person speaking but each is listening for something different.

Taken together, culture can be seen as more than the obvious artifacts of dress, food, language, and religious symbols. At a very deep level, culture is a powerful shaper of our psychology and behavior. It influences the sense of self, the way we process information, what we think is appropriate to feel, how we interpret situations, and what we consider appropriate to express. It is not too large a leap, then, to say that culture influences the ways that we communicate with one another. It can shape norms for gesturing, making eye contact, physical proximity, who gets to speak first in a conversation, and many other aspects of communication, including how we listen. Because Radical Listening is about both sides of the conversation—how we speak and how we listen—it makes sense to dive into the ways that culture affects both of these.

A PRIMER ON CROSS-CULTURAL COMMUNICATION

Once, one of the authors of this book (Robert Biswas-Diener) was running a workshop in London. A discussion of personal strengths was part of the workshop. Robert asked the participants to pair off and discuss a strength that they had recently used. He overheard a man in the front row say, after a period of consideration, "Well, there was one time

I wasn't complete rubbish." This statement is, in many ways, quintessentially British. It carefully avoids any hint of bragging. It would be easy for a foreigner to misconstrue the statement as reflecting low self-esteem. It is easier to interpret if the listener understands that local norms for British reserve and humor can distinctly inform communication.

People who travel, or who work across cultural lines, often encounter puzzling situations related to differences in communication style. There are awkward moments involving tipping, gift giving, compliments, punctuality, physical touch, and so many other topics. The problem is that one person often does not have a cultural script for understanding the other person. They do not know how to decode a statement or behavior because they do not know what cues to look for, what norms apply, or how the other person thinks. This is compounded for people who are conducting business in a non-native language. Imagine how confusing someone might find phrases such as "He's a bit shonky" (Australian English) or "Let's meet at half six" (British English) or "It'll be a slam dunk" (American English) without a little cultural background. The topic of cross-cultural communication is huge—it could (and does) fill whole textbooks. At the risk of oversimplifying, here are six of the most common facets of communication that are heavily influenced by cultural norms (see Table 9.2).

1. Attention to Context

In Japanese culture, there is a concept known as "*ba no kuuki wo yomu*" which translates as "reading the air." A similar concept that English speakers might be familiar with is the notion of "reading the room." In both cases, the idea is that a person is listening to more than just a single speaker. They are intuitively taking the collective pulse; attending to the relative mood of the room, the degree of consensus among those present, and using this information to guide what they say and how they say it. This Japanese concept is a perfect example of the ways that cultures differ in their attention to context.

TABLE 9.2 Facets of cross-cultural communication

Facet of communication	Explanation	Example
Attention to context	Cultures differ in the degree to which—in order to extract meaning—they attend to exactly what is being said versus the context in which it is being said	In some cultures, people are attuned to the relative consensus in the room for a particular idea even though it may not be overtly expressed
Use of non-verbal behaviors	Gaze, smiling, and hand gestures are used differently to communicate concepts or emphasis	In some cultures, you wave someone over with the palm down whereas in others the wave is palm up
Listening norms	Cultures vary in how much they obey turn-based listening versus how much they accept interjection and fast pace	In some cultures, remaining silent is appropriate whereas in others interjecting a joke or finishing the speaker's thought is acceptable
Expressiveness	Cultures vary in which emotions they are comfortable with and how strongly they express emotions	An American might offer exuberant praise to celebrate a successful coworker
Tolerance for conflict	Cultures vary in how straightforward they are in engaging in conflict	In some cultures, people will offer a conditional "yes" or "maybe" when they really mean "no"
Attention to hierarchy	Cultures vary in how much emphasis they place on hierarchy and this emphasis influences speaking and listening	Some people might be more likely to use casual, familiar, or humorous language when speaking to someone who is higher status

So-called low-context cultures, such as Canada, Finland, and the Netherlands, prize straightforwardness and clarity in their messaging. If they had a cultural slogan, it would be "Say what you mean." By contrast, high-context cultures, such as China, Indonesia, and Saudi Arabia, are more likely to emphasize layered and nuanced messaging. It is possible, in these societies, that people will imply their meaning rather than coming right out and stating it explicitly. The distinction between high- and low-context cultures should not be interpreted as one group being more sophisticated in their communication. They are simply different approaches based on a different set of cultural values, assumptions, scripts, and norms.

Erin Meyer, INSEAD professor and author of *The Culture Map*, highlights the point that one approach is not superior to the other.[7] People from tell-it-like-it-is cultures are more likely to think that straightforward communication is a sign of honesty. People in these societies who say exactly what they mean are viewed as more trustworthy whereas those who beat around the bush are seen as less honest. By contrast, people from high-context cultures can feel that the bluntness of straightforward communication can be disrespectful and simplistic. You can see that this is a vital dimension to Radical Listening because it affects not only what you hear (how you direct your attention and notice) but how you hear it (how you interpret and acknowledge it).

2. Non-Verbal Communication

Italians are famous for their hand gestures. There are dozens of them: kissing one's fingertips, making a slicing motion across one's neck, pointing to one's eye, thrusting out an open palm, circling one's ear with a finger, waving, running a thumb across one's cheek, bouncing an upturned hand with the fingers pressed together, rubbing one's chin, and the list goes on. This local sign language conveys meaning on its own or can be used to emphasize what a person says. Without cultural knowledge, however, these expressions remain opaque and confusing.

All cultures—not just Mediterranean ones—rely on hand gestures to communicate meaning. We use our hands as a social shortcut to tell people off, offer directions, express needs such as hunger, remind people of the time, get people's attention, and express satisfaction. Psychologists David Matsumoto and Hyi Sung Hwang have studied gestures across cultures. They found that:[8]

- There are cultural universals: Some gestures—especially around common concepts—are widely used across cultures. For example, "money" is often communicated with a rubbing or tapping of the thumb against the tips of the first two fingers.
- There are divergent meanings of universal gestures: Sometimes the exact same gesture, such as touching the forefinger and thumb together while leaving the other three fingers straight, has very different meanings across cultures. In some cultures, this is a rude gesture whereas in others it means "okay."
- A few gestures are unique to one culture: In Iran, for example, people cover one eye with a palm to convey sincerity.

Non-verbal communication is important because it helps convey meaning or—in the absence of cultural understanding—it can sow confusion. Take, for example, the case of eye contact. People from some East Asian societies have, on average, a lower tolerance for sustained eye contact. When someone from these cultures averts their eyes or looks down, it can be perplexing to Westerners who, in turn, are more likely to interpret sustained eye contact as an indication of engagement in the conversation. One person might be trying to communicate humility or discomfort with a topic whereas the other person is interpreting the interaction as a lack of understanding or interest.

Finally, there is the case of smiling. Cultures differ widely in how frequently they smile, the contexts in which they smile, and the meaning of a smile. *Lonely Planet* guidebooks caution visitors to some nations that smiling can be seen as a sign of stupidity. To investigate this claim, Kuba Krys and his colleagues showed participants from various cultures photos of smiling and unsmiling people and then asked the participants to judge that person's intelligence.[9] Indeed, they found differences in how cultures evaluated a smile. In Germany, for instance, smiling people were viewed as far more intelligent than unsmiling people. In the United States, people ranked intelligence equally regardless of the amount of smiling. In Iran and Japan, by contrast, smiling is associated with lower levels of intelligence. Great listeners use cultural knowledge to notice and interpret more layers of communication, including gestures and expressions.

3. Listening Norms

All conversations, no matter where in the world they occur, include speaking and listening. There are, however, many regional differences. Cultures vary in norms for the pace of conversation, the taking of turns to speak, and how one listens. Researchers have investigated this phenomenon and found distinct ways in which these norms shift from place to place.[10] They include:

- Action: Here, listeners can be more or less active. The least active is remaining silent until the speaker is completely finished. More active approaches include finishing a sentence or thought for the speaker or jumping in with a question even while the speaker is still talking.
- Time: Cultures differ in the pace of conversation. Members of some cultures, for instance, are more likely to feel impatient with long or slow conversations. Similarly, they are more likely to expressly reference time, as in "I only have fifteen minutes to talk."

4. Emotional Expressiveness

Have you ever seen someone spit on the sidewalk in anger? Have you ever seen someone smack another person on the back out of enthusiasm? Have you ever high-fived a stranger or made your face neutral to hide your real feelings? Each of these is an example of the ways that cultures differ in terms of expressiveness. Most often, when we say a person is expressive, we mean that they are emotionally expressive. Whether it is through facial expressions, posture, or gestures, people vary in the extent to which they conceal their feelings or make them transparent.

Social psychologist Shinobu Kitayama has studied emotions, and the ways that they differ across cultures, for decades. He and his colleagues divide the world's cultures into five large zones: Western (e.g., England), East Asian (e.g., Mongolia), South Asian (e.g., India), Arab (e.g., Jordan), and Latin American (e.g., Colombia).[11] Certainly, a case could be made that there are others, such as West African, Sub-Saharan African, and Polynesian, to name just a few. The reason they included these five is because this is where much of the research in psychology has occurred. Of these, there is particularly strong data from three zones: Western, East Asian, and Latin American.

Here is what the Kitayama research team found. People from these distinct cultural groupings differ in the ways that they express emotion. People from Western cultures, for example, are more likely—on average—to express the kinds of emotions that make them distinct and stand out from others, such as pride and anger. This means that listening to the expressed emotion of a Canadian, Australian, or European is listening to a cultural script. Some foreign listeners hear only their own cultural script and so Westerners can come across as brash, self-centered, or full of pride. Being a better cultural listener, however, means hearing the Western script. It is saying, "I am revealing my personal passions to you so that you can know the real me. The ways that I stand out give me meaning, define me, and are even the basis of the contributions I make to the group."

By contrast, people from East Asian cultures are less likely to express emotions in general, and positive emotions such as enthusiasm in particular. For these people, strong emotions are seen as socially disruptive. Interestingly, people from societies such as Japan and Taiwan are more likely than their Western counterparts to experience emotions that promote group harmony, such as guilt. For those wanting to apply a cultural lens to their listening, understanding the East Asian script can be helpful. It says, in essence, "Social harmony is one of the most important things to me. I am willing to hold back my opinions, wants, and emotions so that the group can get along better. My expressions are often about fitting in."

Finally, people from Latin American countries are, like their northern neighbors, more likely to openly express emotions, and this is especially true of positive emotions. They differ from US citizens and Canadians in that their norms seem to center on expressing emotions that are linked to relationships, such as love, affection, respect, compassion, and sympathy. The Latin American script says, "I want to feel connected to you and I want things to be good between us. I hope my positivity has a positive impact on you and on our connection."

5. Tolerance for Conflict

People come into conflict for a shocking number of reasons. We fight over who was first in line, who was first over the line, which dress looks better, which policy will be more effective, which movie had greater artistic merit, who is the greatest guitar player of all time, who owns a piece of land, who invented a piece of technology, and whose turn it is to do the dishes. We can argue over virtually anything and our disagreements range from the most trivial spats to full-blown world wars.

The idea that cultures differ in their tolerance for everyday conflict will likely feel intuitive and familiar. Here, we will put aside major armed conflicts, legal battles, and similar high-stakes disagreements to focus on conflict in everyday interactions: disagreements about business strategy, small arguments over wording, or personality clashes in the office. Typically, we engage in these conflicts on a spectrum from less assertive (avoiding and obliging) to more assertive (collaborating and compromising) to more aggressive (competing and dominating). Where we fall on this continuum is influenced by our cultural norms.

Where Radical Listening is concerned, it is vital to be able to "read" a person's conflict style. Sure, some of it is related to personality, but it is also influenced by their socialization, including their ethnic, religious, class, gender, and linguistic socialization. As a listening shorthand, people from more tight-knit, collectivist cultures tolerate less deviance and disagreement from their members (see Table 9.3). As a result, their norms have evolved to be less openly confrontational. This is why you might hear "I'll look into it" from someone in South Korea who is really saying "Absolutely not!" By contrast, members of individualist cultures are more likely to emphasize straightforward disagreement—openly expressing one's opinion. Many in these cultures relish the opportunity to be the "devil's advocate" in order to present a directly opposing view to the one being presented. Great listeners do not need to adopt an unfamiliar conflict style in order to communicate effectively across cultural divides. However,

TABLE 9.3 Cultural interpretation of conflict styles

	How others can interpret their conflict style	How they can interpret their own conflict style
Collectivists	Ambiguous, dishonest	Accommodating, kind
Individualists	Overbearing, rude	Straightforward, honest

understanding cultural leanings can help them comprehend and accept alternative conflict styles.

6. Attention to Hierarchy

Finally, one important way that cultures differ is in how much stock they place in, and how much they pay attention to, social hierarchy. All cultures have social hierarchy. Queens, prime ministers, CEOs, and university presidents are all widely considered to have more social status than teenagers, college students, housekeepers, or fast-food workers. As evidence of this consider the following: How long would you wait past the appointed meeting time for the leader of your nation? One hour? Three? All day? By contrast, how long would you wait for a high school student who wanted to interview you for their school paper? Not at all? Fifteen minutes? Half an hour?

Where listening is concerned, it can be helpful to understand how a person's culture influences what they say and how they say it. For instance, people who are highly sensitive to hierarchy might be more likely to use honorifics (e.g., using a formal title such as "Dr. Rosenberg"), to use formal language (e.g., removing all slang or swear words), to wait longer for their own turn to speak, or to avoid disagreement with the higher-status person. By contrast, members of other cultures might treat hierarchy more casually, as in the case of a student calling their university professor by their first name, joking around with a high-status person, or using more casual language when interacting.

Early in his teaching career, one of the authors (Christian van Nieuwerburgh) was reprimanded by a school principal for inviting his students to call him by his first name. The school valued hierarchy and formality. In fact, students were expected to stand up when teachers walked into the room and wait until they had been acknowledged before sitting down. Although fun and friendly, Christian's invitation to students would have undermined other figures of authority at the school. Radical Listeners will pay attention to these leanings so that they understand the cultural context for formality or casualness in conversation.

STORY FROM PRACTICE: COMMUNICATING ACROSS CULTURE

Ebbie Gam-Mabatid is the Chief Finance Officer for Pilmico, an international agribusiness company. Their footprint spans eight nations ranging from Vietnam to the Philippines to Brunei. This means that communication across the organization is complicated by differences in time zones, culture, and language. Ebbie understands that the odds are against her where great listening is concerned: her role encourages her to offer advice and directives, she does not share a culture or native language with many of her supervisees, she often has a high-level executive view rather than an on-the-ground understanding of day-to-day operations, and she is decisive which means that she often wants conversations to happen quickly and efficiently. Even so, she knows the power of listening and has worked hard to make better listening part of her leadership style. For example, she has placed "listening ambassadors" in her satellite offices; people who can represent Ebbie but who understand the local culture and language and faithfully translate for her. She works on her own humility so that she does not fall into the temptation of foreclosing on her own ideas at the expense of others' ideas. She encourages storytelling because she understands that narratives can be a rich source of information when they are listened to. She hosts a "CFO dialogue" in which she expects two-way communication with her supervisees and uses these meetings to listen to them. Although these are not perfect strategies, Ebbie feels she has improved as a listener and that it has had a direct effect on company performance.

SUMMARY

Cross-cultural communication is complicated and intriguing. It is a topic that has filled scores of books and countless academic articles. What has already been published offers keen insights into the ways in which people from around the world differ in their communication styles. Radical Listeners harness a basic understanding of these cultural differences to better hear one another. Rather than stumbling over these differences, great listeners use them as context for better appreciating the person to whom they are listening.

QUESTIONS

1. Have you ever been in a cross-cultural misunderstanding? What happened?
2. If you think about culture in terms of psychological qualities, such as identity, tolerance of conflict, and emphasis on hierarchy, what influence does this have on the ways you might listen to others?
3. What, specifically, might you do to prepare to listen better to people from other cultures?

CHAPTER TEN

FERTILE GROUND FOR RADICAL LISTENING

I n 1996, a social service agency made an organization-wide policy change. The leadership decided that it was time to abandon the antiquated notion of command-and-control management and replace it with an employee-first model. Perhaps they had been inspired by a recent training retreat or management bestseller. Whatever the reason, they typed up a memo and distributed it across the organization. In sum, it said that all workers were now mandated to engage in "bottom-up" communication. It is unclear if the leadership understood the irony of this top-down directive. It is one of many examples of well-meaning leaders who want to create a culture that supports great listening and communication but who struggle to do so in practice.

A more successful example can be seen in an initiative launched by Starbucks founder Howard Schultz. In 2008, as the company was growing, Schultz decided to invite the views and perspectives of his customers. To do so, he set up an online platform called "My Starbucks Idea" and invited customers to share suggestions but also to vote and comment on those they had strong opinions about. Starbucks received more than 150,000 ideas that ranged from catering to dietary restrictions to renaming products to themes for advertising. The company made good on its promise to listen well, and a number of these suggestions are now on full display at Starbucks: free Wi-Fi, cake pops, pumpkin spice flavored drinks, splash sticks, and free treats on customer birthdays, to name just a few. The "My Starbucks Idea" program is not listening in the traditional sense of a one-on-one conversation. It does, however, have the hallmarks of Radical Listening in that it asks pertinent questions, pays attention to and acknowledges what is said, and values the speaker.

FERTILE GROUND: A LISTENING INTERVENTION

The purpose of Radical Listening is to have better conversations—allowing people to feel valued, be understood, and believe that they matter. In turn, such conversations foster better human connections that lead to improved relationships. It is easy to think of the skills of listening—paying attention, noticing, remaining quiet, acknowledging, asking questions, and strategically interjecting—as individual behaviors upon which a person can improve. Although this is true, it is not the whole story. A person with amazing listening acumen will still struggle to engage in Radical Listening at a rock concert, in rush hour, or when they are running late. In essence, the environment matters.

In addition to improving your own ability to listen, you can influence your environment so that it supports Radical Listening. Just as a farmer adds fertilizer, you can create metaphorical "fertile ground" for listening. When we use the term "fertile ground," we are referring to environments that are conducive to Radical Listening conversations. This concept includes

- the temporary physical or virtual setting of the conversation (a Zoom call; a meeting room; a shared workspace);

- the cultural milieu (a neighborhood in Mexico City; a seaside town on the Mediterranean; a village in the Swiss Alps; a bustling downtown in South Korea);
- the professional context (a school; a corporate headquarters; a trade show; a charity auction; the factory floor); and
- the corporate culture (formal; laid back; strictly hierarchical).

In recent years, there has been growing interest in the idea of "coaching cultures." Coaching is more than a trendy buzzword; it is a professional role in which one person listens and questions another with the aim of supporting their development. In a "coaching culture," people within an organization adopt this listening-heavy and curiosity-driven way of interacting. There is an intuitive overlap between coaching cultures and Radical Listening. According to Helen Gormley and one of the authors (Christian van Nieuwerburgh), coaching cultures "should motivate individuals and facilitate cooperation, collaboration and connection within the organization and with its external stakeholders."[1]

Creating coaching cultures takes more than simply sending policy memos or organizing a team away day. One of us (van Nieuwerburgh) and a leading coaching psychologist, Jonathan Passmore, proposed that coaching cultures tend to have key characteristics that "create a unique environment for individuals to engage in powerful and meaningful conversations":[2]

- trust
- timely conversations
- possibility of change
- autonomy
- supportive relationships

Developing these characteristics is likely to lead to the creation of fertile ground for Radical Listening (see Figure 10.1).

FERTILE ground

★ TRUST ★

★ TIMELY ★
CONVERSATIONS

POSSIBILITY OF
★ CHANGE ★

★ AUTONOMY ★

SUPPORTIVE
★ RELATIONSHIPS ★

FIGURE 10.1 Cultivating fertile ground
Source: Original artwork by Christian van Nieuwerburgh

Trust

Fertile ground is dependent on high levels of trust between people in a group, team, or organization. In his book, *The Speed of Trust*, Stephen Covey argues that cultivating trust in professional relationships is crucial for success.[3] Of course, "cultivating trust" is easier said than done. Life experience tells us that trust-building takes time. This is because there are two sides to cultivating trust with colleagues.

First, you need to make sure that *you* are trustworthy. There is no point complaining that your colleagues do not share secrets with you if you are the first to share the information with all and sundry. It is necessary to demonstrate through your behavior that you can be trusted. Keeping your promises, protecting confidentiality, and behaving with high levels of integrity will soon bear dividends.

Perhaps the more challenging aspect of cultivating trust is your attitude toward others. If you are suspicious of colleagues, doubt their motives and accuse them of being shifty, trust will remain elusive. Trusting others requires you to assume positive intent and be willing to give people the benefit of the doubt. Yes, you may expose yourself to risk when you do this, but this is the type of vulnerability that will allow you to build trust quickly. Radical Listeners are more likely to be open and trusting in their conversational interactions. This does not mean being naïve. It is simply a case of adopting an open-minded attitude as the starting point for conversations.

Timely Conversations

Fertile ground for Radical Listening depends on people being able to have high-quality conversations *when* they are needed. In other words, Radical Listeners should be available when crucial conversations are required. In practice, this means that your plans should include enough flexibility to allow you to be accessible. When a colleague asks if you have a minute to talk about something urgent, saying "no" runs the risk of damaging the relationship or missing a critical piece of information. Of course, we are not suggesting that you must always drop everything the moment someone asks for a conversation. However, being able to respond positively to a request for a crucial conversation within a reasonable timeframe communicates that you value the other person.

When we have spoken to great listeners in corporate settings, they tell us that these high-quality work-related conversations can sometimes spill over into personal time. Ideally, there should be time available for Radical Listening conversations *during working hours*. This is especially important when we consider the health and well-being of members of the group, team, or organization.

Possibility of Change

Radical Listening conversations are more likely when the people involved believe that change is possible. This allows for more positive conversations that boost hopefulness. Conversations that revolve entirely around complaining about something that is unlikely to change may be well-intentioned, and even feel good, but they rarely lead to better outcomes. In fact, researchers have found that complaining lowers social influence.[4] People working in organizations that are resistant to change are more likely to become cynical and passive. To create fertile ground for Radical Listening, groups, teams, and organizations should be explicit in their openness to change and their desire to achieve even better outcomes. This will create an environment for positive, empowering Radical Listening conversations.

Autonomy

Across industries and roles, people like to have some autonomy at work. In fact, research has linked professional autonomy with higher rates of psychological well-being and self-esteem.[5] What's more, studies reveal that social support and autonomy can increase work engagement.[6]

This means that there will be more opportunities for Radical Listening conversations. Professional autonomy can be increased through leaders empowering others to make decisions, giving people opportunities to lead, providing appropriate development opportunities, and explicitly encouraging creativity and risk-taking.

Supportive Relationships

Groups, teams, and organizations that explicitly emphasize the importance of interconnectedness and good professional relationships are more likely to engage in Radical Listening conversations. There are many ways to do this, from the straightforward articulation of the idea (e.g., "here, we believe that good relationships are central to our success and well-being, and we will do everything we can to invest in them"), to written agreements about ways of working together, to integrating the importance of relationships into strategic plans or vision statements. Essentially, the purpose is to ensure that everyone is encouraged to invest in relationships. Creating an environment in which people are comfortable genuinely showing care about each other, both personally and professionally, is an essential part of the fertile ground necessary for Radical Listening conversations.

THE ROLE OF LEADERS

We have now considered ways of investing in fertile ground by being proactive and intentional. Context is important, and the more we can do to promote the five elements just discussed, the more likely it is that Radical Listening will thrive in your professional context. Having the support of leaders in the organization will fast-track these efforts. If you are one of the leaders, you are well equipped to promote and nurture fertile ground for Radical Listening.

In addition to developing the ability to engage in Radical Listening, you can play an important role in cultivating fertile ground for more of these conversations. Here we consider the significance of leading by example; some listening handicaps to overcome; and the concept of co-creation.

Leading by Example

A commitment to Radical Listening must start at the top of an organization. Unless there is a clear and sustained commitment to Radical Listening from leaders, others are less likely to be fully engaged with the idea. This is, of course, easier said than done. Most leaders would readily endorse the idea that role modeling is an important aspect of setting the cultural tone. Most would also concede that time pressures, shifting trends, and complex work environments can make this difficult.

Leading by example means protecting time for meaningful conversations. It means explicitly promoting the value of such interactions by articulating it in communications throughout the organization. Finally, it means engaging in Radical Listening with a wide range of colleagues. None of this happens easily without leaders prioritizing it. One example can be found in Jens Hofma, the CEO of Pizza Hut in the United Kingdom. Customers and employees of Pizza Hut might be surprised to find Hofma waiting tables at local restaurants. In fact, Hofma works the Pizza Hut floor several hours a week. Is he good at it? No. By his own admission, he is not a great waiter, but he values the experience. Waiting tables allows him to listen in distinct ways: he can overhear the ways that customers talk about the dining experience, he can interact with staff, and he can notice the changing pressures of serving that come with corporate policy changes. This is especially important because Pizza Hut has changed ownership three separate times during Hofma's tenure at the helm.

Admittedly, this is a dramatic example of listening, but it is also why we call this book Radical Listening. We want to underscore the idea that great listening is more than just hearing things or letting others talk. It is the willingness to pay attention, the ability to notice, the desire to ask questions. More than anything, it foregrounds the "why" of listening to others. In this case, Hofma is listening to better understand employee viewpoints and experiences that might otherwise be shielded from him.

Listening Handicaps of Leaders

Even as we are promoting the idea of leading by example, we should acknowledge that leaders have some "handicaps" when it comes to engaging in Radical Listening. Being aware of these handicaps will allow leaders to avoid the negative consequences of each. It makes intuitive sense that there are common, internal barriers to great listening. For example, when a person is only thinking about their own side of the story, or when someone is poised to criticize the speaker's argument, this can interfere with being receptive. Similarly, it makes sense that there are some common environmental obstacles to great listening. When time is short or when there are distractions, people tend to falter in their attention and noticing—two of the critical skills of Radical Listening.

A person's role can also act as context, supporting or interfering with listening. A psychotherapist's role, for instance, places extra emphasis on listening. An organizational leader, by contrast, is likely to experience a few impediments. This is not to suggest that leaders cannot be great listeners—they can. However, there are some predictable obstacles to doing so—we will call these handicaps. Understanding them can be the first step in making certain that leaders nourish fertile ground for Radical Listening through their practices.

1. *The scope handicap.* Leaders, by definition, need to look at the big picture. Because of their high-level view, they sometimes have a hard time listening to people who are describing relatively detailed issues. They are thinking about rolling out an organization-wide

initiative as part of a two-year plan, but the person across the desk from them is describing a technical problem at a single factory. In essence, the two people are speaking different languages. One is fluent in "big picture" and the other in "line work." They need an Esperanto to help them connect. This can be found in the leader's listening agility. Radical Listeners are flexible listeners. They do the mental calculus to determine when knowing about day-to-day operations might be helpful and when it is a distraction. Once they prioritize their conversation partner, they can pay better attention and be more receptive.

2. *The knowledge handicap.* Leaders are often intelligent, expert, and decisive. In fact, leaders sometimes pride themselves on their ability to make good decisions quickly. This is a tendency that often benefits organizations but one that can also interfere with hearing out the ideas of others. Again, great leaders are agile. They have a sense of when to foreclose on an idea and when it is beneficial to receive input and alternatives. Radical Listening, for leaders, is about slowing down long enough to determine the best time for listening and to guard against biases such as falling in love with one's own ideas.

3. *The efficiency handicap.* The pace of business is fast. Many organizations thump their metaphorical chests when they describe the speedy pace at which they work. They love words like "pivot," "deliver," and "leverage;" each of which sounds dynamic. Items that threaten the breakneck pace are often put on the "back burner." This quick tempo is often beneficial to organizations but is not always the friendliest ground for listening. There does not seem to be time to have deep conversations, to question fundamental assumptions, or to solicit multiple views. When leaders engage in Radical Listening, they often slow down, if only temporarily. They realize that time expands and contracts and that the best conversations happen in "slow time" even if they take only fifteen minutes. Remember, the amount of time (how many minutes are used) is qualitatively different than the tempo of the conversation (how rushed or leisurely it feels).

Co-creating the Ideal Environments for Radical Listening

Although leaders have a significant role in cultivating ideal environments for Radical Listening, they cannot do this on their own. Fertile ground should be created collaboratively. One way of doing this is by adopting the concept of "democratic voluntary involvement."[7] In this context, *democratic* means that everyone can see how they would benefit from the fertile ground for Radical Listening. The word *voluntary* reminds us that professionals should not be forced into new initiatives. Leeway should be given for those professionals who engage with change at a slower pace. It would make sense to start by engaging the early adopters and champions. And finally, the word *involvement* relates to allowing anyone interested or excited in the concept of fertile ground to find meaningful ways to engage in the process. The principle of democratic voluntary involvement is important when cultivating fertile ground because the process of co-creating the environment cannot be at odds with the ethos that underpins it.

THE FRUITS OF FERTILE GROUND

If we believe that Radical Listening is a way of building relationships and supporting people to feel valued and seen, we should do what we can to make the environment as conducive for this as possible. The analogy of fertile ground we have been using here comes from a research study on flourishing educators.[8] The researchers were curious about educators who reported that they were flourishing in their schools. Through a series of interviews with teachers, educational leaders, and experts in positive psychology the study was able to identify some of the common factors that led to educators flourishing. Three of the common factors were leaders demonstrating trust; leaders earning trust; and leaders showing an explicit interest in the well-being of educators. This positive environment (fertile ground) which existed in some of the schools led to educators "feeling seen, trusted, and valued" (p. 49). In turn, educators reported that this led to improved relationships, greater authenticity, and professional growth. When used in groups, teams, and organizations, one of the outcomes of Radical Listening conversations is flourishing professionals.

SUMMARY

Radical Listening conversations do not occur in a vacuum. There are millions of conversations happening right now. Each takes place within a specific context. In this chapter, we have highlighted the importance of cultivating environments that are conducive to high-quality conversations. In addition to engaging in Radical Listening, each of us can also have an impact on the personal and professional contexts in which we live and work.

QUESTIONS

1. How will you demonstrate trust in others at the start of Radical Listening conversations?
2. What can you do to make your personal and professional contexts more conducive to Radical Listening conversations?
3. In relation to Radical Listening, what would "leading by example" look like for you?

AFTERWORD

At the close of this journey, we would like to thank you for your engagement and interest in this topic. You have been "listening" to the new ideas, propositions, and provocations in this book. We are grateful to you for this. During the writing process we spent considerable time thinking about you, the reader. We wondered how we could convey our sincere interest in you and the impact that you are going to have through your listening. With this in mind, we would like to tell you more about our intentions and reveal some aspects of our writing strategy. It has always been our intention to provide you with something that is thought-provoking and practical. At the same time, we have tried our best to connect with you, our readers. Books can be a difficult medium for two-way communication because they are so heavily centered around authorial voice. Even so, there are opportunities to forge connections in the same ways that Radical Listening does. One way in which we attempted to connect with you is to talk to you directly, as we are doing here. It is the literary equivalent of eye contact. Another way we approached connection will be largely invisible to you. This book has gone through numerous stages of editing. We spent time considering which aspects of this book might be confronting, confusing, or confining. Where we could not edit these out, we included caveats as a *mea culpa* to acknowledge this. Yet another method of connecting is by including summaries and questions at the end of each chapter. Finally, we included hand-drawn images we created ourselves. It is our hope that these drawings gave the book a more human and personal feel. Here we would like to share with you the final two drawings: an intricate drawing intended to represent the complexity and beauty of Radical Listening (see Figure A.1) and an aide-mémoire of the Radical Listening framework (see Figure A.2).

People are incredibly and delightfully diverse and every context is unique. At the same time, we are all human beings. We all want to

FIGURE A.1 Complexity and beauty
Source: Original artwork by Christian van Nieuwerburgh

QUESTIONING
SUPPLEMENTARY | CONFIRMATORY | EMPHATIC
CELEBRATORY | FUTURE-FOCUSED

INTERJECTIONS
- PROCEDURAL
- EMPHATIC
- STRATEGIC

ASIDES | MINIMAL ENCOURAGERS | HUMOR | ALERTS

ACKNOWLEDGING
JOINING | AFFIRMING | UP-PLAYING | FLATLINING

AWARENESS OF BARRIERS TO LISTENING

LISTENING TO
LISTENING FOR

NOTICING
WHAT IS SAID | HOW IT IS SAID | WHY IT IS SAID

QUIET
- INNER
- CONVERSATIONAL
- ENVIRONMENTAL

ACCEPTING
POINT OF VIEW | SITUATION | PERSONAL LIMITATIONS

RADICAL LISTENING VAN NIEUWERBURGH | BISWAS-DIENER

FIGURE A.2 Aide-mémoire
Source: Original artwork by Christian van Nieuwerburgh

feel valued, be respected, and have opportunities to thrive. We believe that it is possible to support these things through Radical Listening. As authors, we cannot bring about the widespread change we hope to see in the world. We need you to bring these ideas to life through better conversations, better connections, and better relationships. Beyond the pages of this book are countless people waiting to have countless conversations with you. Each and every one of those conversations is an opportunity to acknowledge, to encourage, and to empower.

NOTES

CHAPTER 1

1. "Beyond Distrust: How Americans View Their Government," Pew Research Center (November 23, 2015), https://www.pewresearch.org/politics/2015/11/23/1-trust-in-government-1958-2015/.
2. "Public opinions and social trends, Great Britain: 21 December 2022 to 8 January 2023," Office for National Statistics (January 13, 2023), https://www.ons.gov.uk/peoplepopulationandcommunity/wellbeing/bulletins/publicopinionsandsocialtrendsgreatbritain/21december2022to8january2023#worries-personal-well-being-and-loneliness.
3. "Our Epidemic of Loneliness and Isolation: The U.S. Surgeon General's Advisory on the Healing Effects of Social Connection and Community," Office of the U.S. Surgeon General (2023), https://www.hhs.gov/sites/default/files/surgeon-general-social-connection-advisory.pdf.
4. "As Partisan Hostility Grows, Signs of Frustration with the Two-Party System," Pew Research Center (August 9, 2022), https://www.pewresearch.org/politics/2022/08/09/republicans-and-democrats-increasingly-critical-of-people-in-the-opposing-party/.
5. Lama El Baz and Jinwan Park, "Americans More Concerned about Threats at Home than Abroad," The Chicago Council on Global Affairs (2023).
6. Avraham N. Kluger and Guy Itzchakov, "The Power of Listening at Work," *Annual Review of Organizational Psychology and Organizational Behavior* 9 (2022): 121–46.

7. Karina J. Lloyd, Diana Boer, Joshua Keller, and Sven Voelpel, "Is My Boss Really Listening to Me? The Impact of Perceived Supervisor Listening on Emotional Exhaustion, Turnover Intention, and Organizational Citizenship Behavior," *Journal of Business Ethics* 130 (2015): 509–24.

8. Guy Itzchakov, Avraham Kluger, and Dotan Castro, "I Am Aware of My Inconsistencies but Can Tolerate Them: The Effect of High-Quality Listening on Speakers' Attitude Ambivalence," *Personality and Social Psychology Bulletin* 43 (2017): 105–20.

9. Sigal Shafran Tikva, Avraham Kluger, and Yulia Lerman, "Disruptive Behaviors among Nurses in Israel—Association with Listening, Wellbeing, and Feeling As a Victim: A Cross-Sectional Study," *Israel Journal of Health Policy Research* 8 (2019): 2–9.

10. Avraham N. Kluger and Guy Itzchakov, "The Power of Listening at Work," *Annual Review of Organizational Psychology and Organizational Behavior* 9 (2022): 121–46.

CHAPTER 2

1. Carolyn E. Cutrona and Daniel W. Russell, "Type of Social Support and Specific Stress: Toward a Theory of Optimal Matching," in *Social Support: An Interactional View*, ed. Barbara R. Sarason, Irwin G. Sarason, and Gregory R. Pierce (John Wiley & Sons, 1990).

CHAPTER 3

1. "UK Schoolboy Corrects Nasa Data Error," *BBC News*, March 22, 2017, https://www.bbc.com/news/uk-39351833.

2. Andrew M. Colman, *Oxford Dictionary of Psychology*, 4th ed. (Oxford University Press, 2015).

3. "What Is the Origin of the Phrase 'Pay Attention'?," Stack Exchange, accessed June 30, 2024, https://english.stackexchange.com/questions/388584/what-is-the-origin-of-the-phrase-pay-attention#:~:text=It%20should%20be%20noted%20that,also%20initially%20in%20Great%20Britain.

4. William Shakespeare, *Henry IV, Part 1*, ed. David Bevington (Oxford University Press, 1998).

5. Kevin McSpadden, "You Now Have a Shorter Attention Span Than a Goldfish," *Time*, May 14, 2015, https://time.com/3858309/attention-spans-goldfish/.

6. Gloria Mark, Mary Czerwinski, and Shamsi T. Iqbal, "Effects of Individual Differences in Blocking Workplace Distractions," in *Proceedings of the 2018 CHI Conference on Human Factors in Computing Systems, Montreal, Canada, April 21–26, 2018* (2018), https://doi.org/10.1145/3173574.3173666.

7. Stephen Monsell, "Task Switching," *Trends in Cognitive Sciences* 7, no. 3 (2003): 134–40.

8. Monsell, "Task Switching."

9. Sumi Cho and Eunjoo Lee, "Distraction by Smartphone Use During Clinical Practice and Opinions about Smartphone Restriction Policies: A Cross-Sectional Descriptive Study of Nursing Students," *Nurse Education Today* 40 (2016): 128–33.

10. Peter W. Cardon and Ying Dai, "Mobile Phone Use in Meetings among Chinese Professionals: Perspectives on Multicommunication and Civility," in *Global Advances in Business and Communication Conference and Journal* 3, no. 1 (2014), http://commons.emich.edu/gabc/vol3/iss1/2.

11. David A. Sbarra, Julia L. Briskin, and Richard B. Slatcher, "Smartphones and Close Relationships: The Case for an Evolutionary Mismatch," *Perspectives on Psychological Science* 14, no. 4 (2019): 596–618.

12. Ryan J Dwyer, Kostadin Kushlev, and Elizabeth W. Dunn, "Smartphone Use Undermines Enjoyment of Face-to-Face Social Interactions," *Journal of Experimental Social Psychology* 78 (2018): 233–39.

13. Frances Friedrich, "Attention," in *Noba Textbook Series: Psychology*, ed. Robert Biswas-Diener and Ed Diener (DEF Publishers, 2024), http://noba.to/uv9x8df5.

14. E. C. Cherry, "Some Experiments on the Recognition of Speech, with One and Two Ears," *Journal of the Acoustical Society of America* 25 (1953): 975–79.

15. Neville Moray, "Attention in Dichotic Listening: Affective Cues and the Influence of Instructions," *Quarterly Journal of Experimental Psychology* 11, no. 1 (1959): 56–60.

16. Christopher Chabris and Daniel Simons, *The Invisible Gorilla: How our Intuitions Deceive Us* (Random House, 2011).

17. Alaska White and David O'Hare, "In Plane Sight: Inattentional Blindness Affects Visual Detection of External Targets in Simulated Flight," *Applied Ergonomics* 98 (2022): 103578.

18. Trafton Drew, Melissa L. H. Vo, and Jeremy M. Wolfe, "The Invisible Gorilla Strikes Again: Sustained Inattentional Blindness in Expert Observers," *Psychological Science* 24, no. 9 (2013): 1848–53.

19. Garriy Shteynberg, "A Silent Emergence of Culture: The Social Tuning Effect," *Journal of Personality and Social Psychology* 99, no. 4 (2010): 683–89.
20. Beth Morling, "Shared Attention, Please!," *Noba Blog*, February 10, 2021, http://noba.to/k5h4ryxf.

CHAPTER 4

1. Charles R. Berger, "Speechlessness: Causal Attributions, Emotional Features and Social Consequences," *Journal of Language and Social Psychology* 23, no. 2 (2004): 147–79.
2. Dennis Kurzon, "Towards a Typology of Silence," *Journal of Pragmatics* 39, no. 10 (2007): 1673–88.
3. Alex Gray, "These Are the Cities with the Worst Noise Pollution," *World Economic Forum*, March 27, 2017, https://www.weforum.org/agenda/2017/03/these-are-the-cities-with-the-worst-noise-pollution/.
4. Erin Meyer, *The Culture Map* (Public Affairs, 2014).
5. Mimi Murayama, "Silence: A Comparison of Japanese and US Interpretation" (master's thesis, Portland State University, 1995).
6. Timothy W. Gallwey, *The Inner Game of Tennis: The Classic Guide to the Mental Side of Peak Performance* (Random House Trade Paperbacks, 1997).
7. Mathias Basner, Wolfgang Babisch, Adrian Davis, Mark Brink, Charlotte Clark, Sabine Janssen, and Stephen Stansfeld, "Auditory and Non-Auditory Effects of Noise on Health," *The Lancet* 383, no. 9925 (2014): 1325–32.
8. Deborah Tannen, "Silence: Anything But," in *Perspectives on Silence*, ed. Deborah Tannen and Muriel Saville-Troike (Ablex, 1985).

CHAPTER 5

1. James D. Doorley, Fallon R. Goodman, Kerry C. Kelso, and Todd B. Kashdan, "Psychological Flexibility: What We Know, What We Do Not Know, and What We Think We Know," *Social and Personality Psychology Compass* 14, no. 12 (2020): 1–11.
2. Stefano Boca, Maria Garro, Isabella Giammusso, and Constanza Scaffidi, "The Effect of Perspective Taking on the Mediation Process," *Psychology Research & Behavior Management* 11 (2018): 411–16.
3. Max H. Bazerman, "Judgment and Decision Making," in *Noba Textbook Series: Psychology*, ed. Robert Biswas-Diener and Ed Diener (DEF Publishers, 2024), http://noba.to/9xjyvc3a.

4. Amos Tversky, Daniel Kahneman, and Paul Slovic, eds., *Judgment Under Uncertainty: Heuristics and Biases* (Cambridge University Press, 1982).

5. Daniel Kahneman, Alan B. Krueger, David Schkade, Norbert Schwarz, and Arthur A. Stone, "Would You be Happier if You Were Richer? A Focusing Illusion," *Science* 312, no. 5782 (2006): 1908–10.

6. Tore Pedersen, Per Kristensson, and Margareta Friman, "Counteracting the Focusing Illusion: Effects of Defocusing on Car Users' Predicted Satisfaction with Public Transport," *Journal of Environmental Psychology* 32, no. 1 (2012): 30–36.

7. Tenelle Porter, Abdo Elnakouri, Ethan A. Meyers, Takuya Shibayama, Eranda Jayawickreme, and Igor Grossmann, "Predictors and Consequences of Intellectual Humility," *Nature Reviews Psychology* 1, no. 9 (2022): 524–36.

8. Mark R. Leary, Kate J. Diebels, Erin K. Davisson, Katrina P. Jongman-Sereno, Jennifer C. Isherwood, Kaitlin T. Raimi, Samantha A. Deffler, and Rick H. Hoyle, "Cognitive and Interpersonal Features of Intellectual Humility," *Personality and Social Psychology Bulletin* 43, no. 6 (2017): 793–813.

9. Tenelle Porter, Abdo Elnakouri, Ethan A. Meyers, Takuya Shibayama, Eranda Jayawickreme, and Igor Grossmann, "Predictors and Consequences of Intellectual Humility," *Nature Reviews Psychology* 1, no. 9 (2022): 524–36.

10. Ethan A. Meyers, Martin H. Turpin, Michał Białek, Jonathan A. Fugelsang, and Derek J. Koehler, "Inducing Feelings of Ignorance Makes People More Receptive to Expert (Economist) Opinion," *Judgment and Decision Making* 15, no. 6 (2020): 909–25.

11. Tenelle Porter, and Karina Schumann, "Intellectual Humility and Openness to the Opposing View," *Self and Identity* 17, no. 2 (2018): 139–62.

12. Todd B. Kashdan, Paul Rose, and Frank D. Fincham, "Curiosity and Exploration: Facilitating Positive Subjective Experiences and Personal Growth Opportunities," *Journal of Personality Assessment* 82, no. 3 (2004): 291–305.

CHAPTER 6

1. John M. Gottman, James Coan, Sybil Carrere, and Catherine Swanson, "Predicting Marital Happiness and Stability from Newlywed Interactions," *Journal of Marriage and the Family* 60 (1998): 5–22.

2. John Gottman and Nan Silver, *The Seven Principles for Making Marriage Work: A Practical Guide from the Country's Foremost Relationship Expert* (Three Rivers Press, 1999).

3. Shelly L. Gable, Harry T. Reis, Emily A. Impett, and Evan R. Asher, "What Do You Do When Things Go Right? The Intrapersonal and Interpersonal Benefits of Sharing Positive Events," *Journal of Personality and Social Psychology* 87, no. 2 (2004): 228–45.

CHAPTER 7

1. Gordon Wood, "The Knew-It-All-Along Effect," *Journal of Experimental Psychology: Human Perception and Performance* 4, no. 2 (1978): 345–53.

CHAPTER 8

1. Daniel J. Wakin, "Ringing Finally Ended, but There's No Button to Stop Shame," *New York Times*, January 12, 2012, https://www.nytimes.com/2012/01/13/nyregion/ringing-finally-stopped-but-concertgoers-alarm-persists.html.
2. Deborah James and Sandra Clarke, "Women, Men, and Interruptions: A Critical Review," in *Gender and Conversational Interaction*, ed. Deborah Tannen (Oxford University Press, 1993), 231–80.
3. Lynn Smith-Lovin and Charles Brody, "Interruptions in Group Discussions: The Effects of Gender and Group Composition," *American Sociological Review* 54 (1989): 424–35.
4. Ilona Plug, Sandra van Dulmen, Wyke Stommel, Tim C. olde Hartman, and Enny Das, "Physicians' and Patients' Interruptions in Clinical Practice: A Quantitative Analysis," *The Annals of Family Medicine* 20, no. 5 (2022): 423–29.
5. David Peterson, Zoom conversation with Robert Biswas-Diener, July 19, 2021.
6. Erin Meyer, *The Culture Map* (Public Affairs, 2014).
7. Deborah Tannen, "New York Jewish Conversational Style," *International Journal of the Sociology of Language* 30 (1981): 133–50.
8. Deborah Tannen, "In Real Life, Not All Interruptions Are Rude," *New York Times*, September 25, 2021, https://www.nytimes.com/2021/09/25/opinion/interrupting-cooperative-overlapping.html.
9. Kumiko Murata, "Intrusive or Co-operative? A Cross-Cultural Study of Interruption," *Journal of Pragmatics* 21, no. 4 (1994): 385–400.
10. Christian van Nieuwerburgh, *An Introduction to Coaching Skills: A Practical Guide*, 3rd ed. (Sage, 2021).
11. Tannen, "New York Jewish Conversational Style."

CHAPTER 9

1. George Stricker and Steven J. Trierweiler, "The Local Clinical Scientist. A Bridge between Science and Practice," *American Psychologist* 50, no. 12 (1995): 995–1002.

2. Robert Biswas-Diener and Neil Thin, "Culture," in *Noba Textbook Series: Psychology*, ed. Robert Biswas-Diener and Ed Diener (DEF Publishers, 2024), http://noba.to/y9xcptqw.

3. Harry Triandis, *Individualism and Collectivism (New Directions in Social Psychology)*, 1st ed. (Taylor and Francis, 1995); Eunkook M. Suh, "Self, the Hyphen between Culture and Subjective Well-Being," in *Culture and Subjective Well-Being*, ed. Ed Diener and Eunkook M. Suh (MIT Press, 2000).

4. Shinobu Kitayama and Hazel Rose Markus, eds. *Emotion and Culture: Empirical Studies of Mutual Influence*, 1st ed. (American Psychological Association, 1994); Robert Biswas-Diener, Louis Tay, and Ed Diener, "Happiness in India," in *Happiness Across Cultures*, ed. Helaine Selin and Gareth Davey, vol. 6 (Springer, 2012).

5. Richard Nisbett, *The Geography of Thought: How Asians and Westerners Think Differently . . . and Why* (Free Press, 2003).

6. Nisbett, *The Geography of Thought*.

7. Erin Meyer, *The Culture Map* (Public Affairs, 2014).

8. David Matsumoto and Hyi Sung Hwang, "Cultural Influences on Nonverbal Behavior," in *Nonverbal Communication: Science and Applications*, ed. David Matsumoto, Mark G. Frank and Hyi Sung Hwang (Sage Publications, 2013).

9. Kuba Krys, Karolina Hansen, Cai Xing, Piotr Szarota, and Miao-miao Yang, "Do Only Fools Smile at Strangers? Cultural Differences in Social Perception of Intelligence of Smiling Individuals," *Journal of Cross-Cultural Psychology* 45, no. 2 (2014): 314–21.

10. Christian Kiewitz, James B. Weaver III, Hans-Bernd Brosius, and Gabriel Weimann, "Cultural Differences in Listening Style Preferences: A Comparison of Young Adults in Germany, Israel, and the United States," *International Journal of Public Opinion Research* 9, no. 3 (1997): 233–47.

11. Shinobu Kitayama and Cristina E. Salvador, "Cultural Psychology: Beyond East and West," *Annual Review of Psychology* 75 (2024): 495–526.

CHAPTER 10

1. Helen Gormley and Christian van Nieuwerburgh, "Developing Coaching Cultures: A Review of the Literature," *Coaching: An International Journal of Theory, Research and Practice* 7, no. 2 (2014): 90–101.

2. Christian van Nieuwerburgh and Jonathan Passmore, "Creating Coaching Cultures for Learning," in *Coaching in Education: Getting Better Results for Students, Educators and Parents*, ed. Christian van Nieuwerburgh (Karnac, 2012), 153–72.

3. Stephen M. R. Covey, *The Speed of Trust: The One Thing That Changes Everything* (Free Press, 2011).

4. Michal Bialek and Artur Domurat, "Complaining Decreases the Efficacy of Dialogue as a Method of Social Influence," *Management and Business Administration* 23 (2015): 32–48.

5. Donald G. Gardner, "The Importance of Being Resilient: Psychological Well-being, Job Autonomy and Self-Esteem of Organization Managers," *Personality and Individual Differences* 155 (2020): 109731.

6. Sakari Taipale, Kirsikka Selander, Timo Anttila, and Jouko Nätti, "Work Engagement in Eight European Countries: The Role of Job Demands, Autonomy, and Social Support," *International Journal of Sociology and Social Policy* 31, no. 7/8 (2011): 486–504.

7. Christian van Nieuwerburgh, "Towards a Coaching Culture" in *Coaching in Professional Contexts*, ed. Christian van Nieuwerburgh (Sage Publications, 2016), 227–34.

8. Brittany Rehal and Christian van Nieuwerburgh, "Understanding the Factors that Contribute to Educator Flourishing," *International Journal of Wellbeing* 12, no. 2 (2022): 36–87.

ACKNOWLEDGMENTS

T his book is not the product of two coauthors. It takes a team to usher a book to market and most of those involved work behind the scenes. It began as a discussion of possible book topics at lunch one day with Sarah Nelson and Neal Maillet. We are especially indebted to Neal for championing this book and for his editorial attention throughout the process. Thanks also to Ashley Ingram for her inspiring cover design. There is little question that the current version of this book is stronger than earlier drafts thanks to the careful reviews offered by Jill Swenson, Cheryl Curtis, and Megan Prentiss. We would like to thank the entire team at Berrett-Koehler for helping make *Radical Listening* a reality.

We relied on the indispensable Nadezhda (Nadia) Lyubchik to help us organize our thinking and the references. Jim Knight has provided sage counsel and encouragement to CvN throughout the process. Karen Guggenheim should also be mentioned here because she gave RBD a platform to present a keynote on listening by which we could test some of our early thinking that formed the foundation of this book.

INDEX

Bold page ranges indicate primary discussion of topic.

ABOUT THE AUTHORS

Prof. Christian van Nieuwerburgh (PhD) is a leading academic and executive coach. He is Professor of Coaching and Positive Psychology at RCSI University of Medicine and Health Sciences (Ireland) and Principal Fellow at the Centre for Wellbeing Science of the University of Melbourne (Australia). Christian delivers consultancy, training, and executive coaching globally, regularly presenting in the United States, the United Kingdom, Europe, Australia, New Zealand, and the Middle East. He is passionate about motorcycling, writing, and coaching. Find out more on coachonamotorcycle.com.

Dr. Robert Biswas-Diener is a well-being researcher with seventy-five academic publications. He has shared his expertise in keynotes and workshops in thirty nations. Robert is also widely recognized as a pioneer of positive psychology coaching and is passionate about training ethical and effective coaches. His previous book, *Positive Provocation*, was shortlisted for the Thinkers50 Coaching and Mentoring Award. Robert lives in Portland, Oregon, where he enjoys drawing, rock climbing, and cats.

Berrett–Koehler
Publishers

Berrett-Koehler is an independent publisher dedicated to an ambitious mission: *Connecting people and ideas to create a world that works for all.*

Our publications span many formats, including print, digital, audio, and video. We also offer online resources, training, and gatherings. And we will continue expanding our products and services to advance our mission.

We believe that the solutions to the world's problems will come from all of us, working at all levels: in our society, in our organizations, and in our own lives. Our publications and resources offer pathways to creating a more just, equitable, and sustainable society. They help people make their organizations more humane, democratic, diverse, and effective (and we don't think there's any contradiction there). And they guide people in creating positive change in their own lives and aligning their personal practices with their aspirations for a better world.

And we strive to practice what we preach through what we call "The BK Way." At the core of this approach is *stewardship,* a deep sense of responsibility to administer the company for the benefit of all of our stakeholder groups, including authors, customers, employees, investors, service providers, sales partners, and the communities and environment around us. Everything we do is built around stewardship and our other core values of *quality, partnership, inclusion,* and *sustainability.*

This is why Berrett-Koehler is the first book publishing company to be both a B Corporation (a rigorous certification) and a benefit corporation (a for-profit legal status), which together require us to adhere to the highest standards for corporate, social, and environmental performance. And it is why we have instituted many pioneering practices (which you can learn about at www.bkconnection.com), including the Berrett-Koehler Constitution, the Bill of Rights and Responsibilities for BK Authors, and our unique Author Days.

We are grateful to our readers, authors, and other friends who are supporting our mission. We ask you to share with us examples of how BK publications and resources are making a difference in your lives, organizations, and communities at www.bkconnection.com/impact.

Dear reader,

Thank you for picking up this book and welcome to the worldwide BK community! You're joining a special group of people who have come together to create positive change in their lives, organizations, and communities.

What's BK all about?

Our mission is to connect people and ideas to create a world that works for all.

Why? Our communities, organizations, and lives get bogged down by old paradigms of self-interest, exclusion, hierarchy, and privilege. But we believe that can change. That's why we seek the leading experts on these challenges—and share their actionable ideas with you.

A welcome gift

To help you get started, we'd like to offer you a **free copy** of one of our bestselling ebooks:

www.bkconnection.com/welcome

When you claim your **free ebook**, you'll also be subscribed to our blog.

Our freshest insights

Access the best new tools and ideas for leaders at all levels on our blog at ideas.bkconnection.com.

Sincerely,

Your friends at Berrett-Koehler